Day To Day Secrets

Eugene Fullerton

authorHOUSE®

AuthorHouse™ UK Ltd.
500 Avebury Boulevard
Central Milton Keynes, MK9 2BE
www.authorhouse.co.uk
Phone: 08001974150

First published by AuthorHouse 4/23/2009

ISBN: 978-1-4389-5909-2 (sc)

This book is printed on acid-free paper.

Foreword.

This second book of poems from July to December was one of the biggest challenges in my life. To find new material everyday is a lot more difficult than I ever imagined. Trying not to repeat myself meant that I had to try and block out the day before and to focus on something completely new and different each day.

I have to say the completion of this book is the result of many hours of mind-searching and writing. However, I must say to see the final completion has been a satisfying reward

. E.F.

Dedications.

I would like to dedicate this second book to all the medical and surgical staff of Craigavon Area Hospital. Their commitment and devotion to myself during my illness deserves great praise and thanks. In fact words would be inadequate to describe their kindness and skill. I wish them all happiness and fulfilment in the years ahead.

~~~~~~~~~~~~~~~~

A special word of thanks to my wife Winifred and my daughter Joanne for their help in the production of this book.

~~~~~~~~~~~~~~~~

Cover picture by Joanne Fullerton:
Fraser Island, Brisbane, Australia.

July

Titles of Poems	*Month of July*		
July Showers	1st July	Tuesday	2008
Aghaderg Parish	2nd July	Wednesday	2008
Breakfast Time	3rd July	Thursday	2008
Gone Deaf	4th July	Friday	2008
Your Lot	5th July	Saturday	2008
Look At Me	6th July	Sunday	2008
Neighbours	7th July	Monday	2008
My Son	8th July	Tuesday	2008
The Bann	9th July	Wednesday	2008
Grasp The Moment	10th July	Thursday	2008
Parish Priest	11th July	Friday	2008
The Glorious Twelfth	12th July	Saturday	2008
Sham Fight	13th July	Sunday	2008
Nothing Matters	14th July	Monday	2008
Perseverance	15th July	Tuesday	2008
Darkie Dog	16th July	Wednesday	2008
Right Choice	17th July	Thursday	2008
Race To White House	18th July	Friday	2008
The Big Screen	19th July	Saturday	2008
Blazing Corpse	20th July	Sunday	2008
Turn The Clock Back	21st July	Monday	2008
Ballyvarley Ghost	22nd July	Tuesday	2008
Flax Pulling	23rd July	Wednesday	2008
The Billy Goat	24th July	Thursday	2008

July Showers.

1ˢᵗ July Tuesday 2008.

July has sprung upon us
and we're singing in the rain,
With umbrellas open
we have reasons to complain,
For every drop that falls at speed
and dances on the ground,
There's rivers flowing down the lawn
no dry place to be found.

It's just the climate in this place
a verse or two you'd hear,
It's just the month were living in
at this oul time of year,
You're sure to get this weather
when it's holiday time again,
Now were two weeks off the work
You'll be sure to get the rain.

So that is why were heading off
to get the summer sun,
We're going to Barcelona
to have ourselves some fun,
So we don't care about July
it can rain all night and day,
For the next two weeks of summer
we'll be sunning far away.

Aghaderg Parish.

2nd July Wednesday 2008.
The town land that I live in is one of twenty eight
Connected to this parish I will try to illustrate,
The name of our wee Parish christened many years ago
It is Achadh Leith Dheirg in Irish
But Aghaderg is what we know.

Now it stretches seven miles plus one half from Glaskermore,
and it ends up in Drumiller, I have more for you in store,
It is five miles wide from Caskum,
to where it ends in Lisnagade,
Loughadian, Legananny, Lisnagonnell,
 Lisnatierny, Lisnabrague.

Ballyvarley, Ballygowan, Bovennett, and Ballynaskeagh,
Ballinataggart and the Brickland, takes us slightly past halfway,
Then it's on to Carrickdrumman,, there is Creevy, Coolnacran,
Derrydrummuck, and Drumsallagh,
~~Drumalane~~ make up this land.
Drumnahare

Glaskerbeg is broke in two one is east and one is west
There is Greenan there is Meenan,
put Glenloughlan with the rest,
Well by now you will have noticed in my efforts to fulfil
That I have left out Scarva, and of course there is Shan-kill.

Aghaderg is approximately 7.5 miles x 5 miles = 37.5 sq miles

With 640 acres to the sq mile x 37.5 then Aghaderg covers =
Approx 24000 thousand acres.

The Parish of Aghaderg (The Red Field)
goes back to the year 332

Breakfast time.

Early in the morning, at my breakfast sitting down
I recall some precious moments, you and I had all around
In the walls there made of silence
I can hear the rafters roar,
With the children singing merrily
"The Streets of Baltimore"

And every time I lift the spoon reminds me of those days,
Sitting in their high chairs feeding them in different ways,
And even though the most of it
direction wise was good,
It was hard to save the floor
from eating some cold baby food.

No matter when the clock went off
or the rooster made its cry,
Cause usually then the most of them
flew round like butterflies,
For in their minds they always thought
when dark you go to bed
And when it's bright and early
your wings you have to spread.

And so it does remind me when at breakfast we sit down
Of all those early mornings, hearing super sonic sounds,
Where every door was exercised,
light switches off and on,
you never could imagine it
when those wee things were born.

Gone Deaf.

4th July Friday 2008.

Sometimes in the evening when I think that I've gone deaf
I take myself down to the rooms and there I draw my breath,
For lying there like sparrows
with their squawking now much lower,
I find it's at this time of day
I truly love them more.

For sometimes during the hours of day
when they are in full bloom,
The levels of the noise increases out of every room,
You could even be forgiven
for your thoughts of going mad,
For a quick supply of earplugs
you certainly would be glad.

Now it's not that they'd be crying
or fighting with each other,
It's just they seemed to constantly
talk loud to one another,
For out of these little diaphragms
these bursts of noise were heard,
Till finally you had
to gather up these humming birds.

But mostly, alas it never ever came to be
Their little tongues could not be held,
of that I guarantee.
But when you come to think of it
you have to bow your head,
There are many parents nowadays
who do not have that dread.

Your Lot.

Some say life is democratic
that everybody gets their turn,
Three score and ten to the big 'Amen'
after that it's of no concern.

Maybe that's true to a certain extent
because you have to leave it all behind,
It makes no difference what you own
that's the way this life is designed.

Now no-one is responsible for being born
so you can't take that on board,
You cannot burden yourself with that
it's an oppression you cannot afford.

But to say it's democratic I couldn't be sure
for some are more privileged than others,
And some will get through albeit a few
who aren't too concerned with their brothers.

So maybe it's fair, in this life to share
that all of us get a good chance,
Whilst many improve with the talents they use
there are those who just never advance.

But life is so strange, it's a mystery to us
regarding the time we have here,
For many die young, they have only begun

some celebrate, <u>One Hundred Years.</u>

Look at Me.

6th July Sunday 2008.

Look at me today Lord
What do you see?
A broken body, Just a shadow of me
A stitched up frame of the person I was,
No rhyme or reason
Just a time to pause.

Look at me today Lord
What do you see?
A broken spirit, all ready to flee,
With scars on my body,
and wounds on my flesh,
Bones that were broken
All swollen and threshed.

I look at you today son
And what do I see?
A broken body, that resembles me,
A stitched up frame, of the person you were,
No rhyme or reason
But my son I care.

I look at you today son
What do I see?
A broken spirit, just waiting for me,
With scars on your body,
and wounds on your flesh,
Bones that were broken
I will heal them up fresh.

Neighbours.

7th July Monday 2008.

If you head out from Jinglers Bridge,
In the centre of Banbridge Town,
And travel out the Scarva Road
For approximately two and half miles,
You will stop in Ballyvarley
A town land you all should know,
Where people live in harmony
And friendships always grow.

It is long since I was born there
In nineteen fifty two,
And I always can remember
How the neighbours were like glue,
For they always stuck together
And they helped each other out,
They knew their Christian values
And what life was all about.

Now their doors were always open
And their hands were just the same,
You could ask to borrow sugar
Without being put to shame,
There was a feeling of contentment
When you shared some eggs around,
And you got a pound of butter
In return you always found.

In all the years that have disappeared up to this present day
This place it hasn't changed much to be truthful I can say,
For the people you will find, are still generous and kind
Living out in Ballyvarley a few miles from Banbridge town.

My Son.

8th July Tuesday 2008.

I remember the day you took the car away
you had only passed your test some time before,
And you were all siked up with joy
and excitement with this toy,
Unfamiliar with the dangers I implore.

Well, I can still recall, giving you an overhaul
to remind you of the risks out on the road,
So remember what I said
keep them tightly in your head,
And observe the rules you learned,
the Highway Code.

But my words they were in vain
when a phone call to explain,
Said the car was on its roof way down the road.
And when I arrived on site
I refrained with all my might,
for my angry feelings wanted to explode.

Now the car was in bad shape
but he managed to escape
and he only had a gash above his eye,
He was standing on the ground,
so ashamed he'd let me down
but I was so relieved he was still alive.

The Bann.

9th July Wednesday 2008.

When you're standing in the centre of dear old Banbridge town
Just listen for a moment and you will hear the sound,
Flowing from the mountains high in the Mournes it all began
You'll hear the gurgling waters of the rippling river Bann.

The Bann it pushes forward to its home there in Lough Neagh
It leaves the point of White Coat, Spelga Valley every day,
Close to Hilltown and past Katesbridge,
And then through Banbridge town,
Through industries of linen, Gilford Mill, then Portadown.

Now down the years this River Bann of 80 miles has flowed
It must be disappointed just to see the factories closed,
For once it witnessed linen sheets spread white on either side,
And turned the mighty Mill wheels
to keep factory power supplied.

Repeat second verse as chorus.

Then forward on its journey from Portadown it flows
Where anglers test their deftness, Hoys meadows they will go,
Then finally it winds up close to Maghery at Bannfoot
Where a hand rope ferry used to work
Is now closed up and shut.

Repeat the Chorus again

The Bann it pushes forward to its home their in Lough Neagh
It leaves the point of Whitecoat, Spelga valley every day,
Close to Hilltown and past Katesbridge
And then through Banbridge town,
Through industries of linen , Gilford Mill then Portadown.

Grasp the Moment.

10th July Thursday 2008.

Nothing beats the moment we call 'Now'
There is no time like the present I can vow,
Don't put off until tomorrow
What you can do today,
You will find it's worth the bother anyhow.

If you decide there are things you need to do
Then take a pen and plan it all for you,
Don't keep putting it on hold
Just allow it to unfold,
You will feel much better when you're in control.

If there's someone sick that you would like to see
But you hesitate and say you'll let it be,
Then it's likely you'll be late
You'll be in an awful state,
Use your instincts keep your visits up to date.

Now you know yourself you'd like to give a hand
For some charity or other you could plan,
It would always be worthwhile
Introduce a brand new smile,
And encourage someone else to join the clan.

Sometimes it's very hard to make a move
No matter how you think things will improve,
But unless you grasp the moment when you can
It could pass you by and not return again.

Parish Priest.

11th July Friday 2008.

"Now the preacher preaches far too long
and he sends us all to sleep",
But when he cuts it very short
They say his efforts cheap.

And then his voice is far too loud, it rises up when praying,
But when he tones it down a bit
"You can't hear what he's saying."

If he goes on holidays "he's always on the road"
If he's going nowhere then "he's starting to corrode",
"He's never off the batter"
when he visits some ones house,
And when he doesn't bother
He's accused of being a mouse.

When he mentions money
they could run him out of town,
If he doesn't spend it, then "the place is all run down",
If he's running round the parish, then he gets in peoples heads
If he's simply doing nothing, then "the parish it is dead".

If the parish priest is far too young
then "sure what would that man know?"
And if he is too old to work, then "it's time that he should go",
And in the end when the poor man dies
He can never fall from grace,
"For there was nobody like him

And no one could fill his place!"

The Glorious Twelfth.

12th July Saturday 2008.

On the twelfth of July
as it yearly comes round,
There's mass celebrations
in country and towns,
Where men in orange sashes
and bowlers of black,
They walk in possession
behind others backs.

Now they corner the highways
to further their cause,
From Summer to Autumn
they march to applause,
They meet in the fields
to be watered and fed,
And listen to speeches
from oul figureheads.

And then in the evenings
some drink themselves dry,
And turn to their comrades
to wish them goodbye,
They wait for the day
to return once again,
To hammer the streets
with their drum beats descend.

Sham Fight.

13th July Sunday 2008.

He went to Scarva every year
and took his gear and all,
He picked himself a lovely spot
and there set up his stall.

A picture of the pope he had
and a forty gallon drum,
"You give his holiness a kick.
flick a pound in with your thumb",

Now every year the barrel was full,
he'd lift this great amount,
The crack was good, as was the mood
and the cash was hard to count.

Well now one year it ended,
and this lad became a man,
"The Sham fight for me is over
for I've done all I can".

We've counted up the money
and we're loaded to the hilt,
Now I know it was expensive
but we got the Chapel built!

Nothing Matters.

14ᵗʰ July Monday 2008.

Nothing matters when you're born
Except your mothers breast,
Cuddle in and suck away
And she will do the rest.

Nothing matters when you're sober
Except you need a drink,
Tell yourself you're not concerned
And don't care what others think.

Nothing matters when you're drunk
Except the bottle open,
Stammer, stutter all you like
But drink up more you're hoping.

Nothing matters when you're down
Except the fact you're on the ground,
You can choose to stay there stuck
Or make the effort to rebound.

Nothing matters when you're dead
Except where you are going,
Just be careful who you meet
Especially if he's glowing.

Perseverance

15th July Tuesday 2008.

Is there a limit to this work that I can do
To these poems that I write,
Are there restrictions to my thoughts
Is there an end in sight.

What can I do for new ideas to keep me writing
To keep this pen in hand,
Is there I limit to a conversation then
Or can I wave a magic wand.

Well there is a simple answer, just for me to grab
And store in my computer made of flesh,
For every time I speak, or utter two more words
I have thought of something different, something fresh.

So importantly for me I must keep scrawling
And record most every concept in my head,
But the crucial thing for me that I keep fighting
Is to write it down before I go to bed.

For most of what comes in one ear has bother
Taking hold of in between my human brain,
In fact the most of it goes out the other
And leaves it totally empty like a drain.

So commitment, dedication and devotion
In the end will fill these arduous months for me,
I will have to find the total inclination

That will take me to December,   Finally.

Darkie Dog.

It was Grand National day and my Uncle Dan was calling,
I'd already picked a horse for him, with a pin,
Eyes closed, down the page crawling.

Red Alligator was my choice for him, two shillings each way
I thought he could afford more,
But for him it was a one off on the day.

He was only through the gate, complaining
That a dog was at his sheep,
Well my dog was in his house, as I thought, fast asleep,

When suddenly round the gable came Darkie
A baby lamb tucked neatly in his jaws,
The world stopped for me, disappointed
For I thought my dog was indoors.

My father angrily grabbed my dog by the collar
And removed the lamb, a lifeless body dripping with blood,
"You're in big trouble now son, this dog is for the chop
And believe me you are in the mud".

I looked at Dan, my father's brother-in-law
My Uncle by marriage, he surely would not
Inflict punishment on my dog … would he?
Stumbling I said, "I picked your horse for today
Red Alligator he will win, I know I can guarantee".

Little did I know that he would make a swap
And lucky for me, in a few hours time
My dog was free.

Right Choice.

17ᵗʰ July Thursday 2008.

I don't know what I would do without you
You are my balustrade the one I lean against,
You keep me from falling over the top,
The one for me who makes the most sense.

They say there's a very good woman
Behind every successful man's life,
Be sure there's no prizes for guessing
For its usually this fortunate mans wife.

Now be careful when picking and choosing
Don't go for looks strictly alone,
But look for a mixture of beauty
And one who can run a good home.

For having someone to come home too
Who can solidly stand by your side,
Will give you a great sense of freedom
Of confidence, assurance and pride.

So guard and protect your investment
Your shares and your interest will grow,
You will never regret this decision
All you need is the wisdom to know.

Race to White House.

18th July Friday 2008.

Will it make any difference
 a new man in the White House,
Does it really matter if he's black or white,
For they all read speeches
from other peoples writing,
So do they care that much, if they're wrong or right.

Well at this present time he will need to shine
And he will need to lead the way,
But not in the sense that leads to War
He will need to reflect and pray.

But this will not be easy for whoever gets the job,
For you cannot please all people
and not every one will absorb,
For one will say that conflicts right
to justify the wrongs,
While others say it's never right
So the arguments are strong.

So if it is Obama or Senator John Mc Cain
we wish them both success,
But will they make a difference
for now we can only Guess.

The Big Screen.

19th July Saturday 2008.

I used to love the westerns, I watched when I was young
But I find as I get older, that my interests they have sprung,
For I do not have the patience now, to let myself be fooled
And yet I just admire those men their acting was so cool.

Now I admired Lee Marvin, Clint Eastwood and John Wayne,
Bob Mitchim, and Kirk Douglas and Alan Ladd in Shane,
Burt Lancaster was my favourite, Gunfight OK corrall,
Henry Fonda he was special the outlaws he shot them all.

James Stewart and Maralin Brando,
The two Anthony's Quinn and Quayle
James Coburn and George Kennedy all put villains in their jails,
Now Van Heflin and Jack Palance, they also starred in Shane,
Gregory Peck and Audie Murphy, all rode the rough terrain,
Charlton Heston, Richard Widmark,
Steve Mc Queen and Lee Van cleef,
Robert Taylor, Robert Fuller, Randolph Scott, Omar Sharrif.

And then there's Eli Wallagh, Jimmy Cagney, Lee J cobb,
Humphrey Bogart, Robert Redford,
Stephen Boyd, Gathered up the mob
Well there's twisty eye Jack Elam, Jason Roberts, Robert Stack,
Paul Newman, and Rod Stieger, with Karl Maldon in the pack,
Earl Flynn and Richard Harris, Robert Gulp and Orson Welles
James Cann and Ernest Borgnine, they all sent men to hell.

Well the Searchers was my favourite,
Ward Bond he was the best,
The big Country it was brilliant Burl Ives up with the Rest,
I also liked Charles Bronson and wee Robinson Edward G,

They all adorned the big screen as large as life could BE.

Blazing Corpse.

20th July Sunday 2008.

An oul fellow sat on a chair at a wake
Just patiently waiting to get a wee spake,
But as he would think of a few words to make
Some other oul doll she would open her bake.

So he twisted and turned and puffed on his pipe
And he gazed at the people there different types,
He thought to himself as he sat there that night,
Just what he could do to give them a fright.

Now as he sat tight in the chair like a mouse,
The sound in the place it was like a hen house,
So he walked to the corpse to try and arouse
He slipped some tobacco on the front of his blouse.

Well soon it would seem, the corpse went to hell,
The women were screaming and feeling unwell,
And soon they were leaving each one with a yell
With a bucket of water
he quenched down the smell.

Very soon it was quiet he said a wee prayer
Uninterrupted, he was the only one there,
Since no one their voices were willing to share
He decided to sit on his own in the chair.

Turn The Clock Back.

21st July Monday 2008.

If I could turn the clock back
And live my life again,
It almost is a certainty
I'd do it all the same,
I know it would be different
The first time wasn't planned
But I think I'd just repeat it
And end up this type of man.

For I know it wasn't perfect
And there's things
I could have changed,
But learning is a process
Looking back you can't explain,
But comparing it with others
You just come to realize,
There were gifts of many blessings
You just have to recognize.

So if I could turn the clock back
And live my life again,
I would start a little earlier
To give thanks and say amen,
But since it is too late for that
I think I'll start right now,
And whisper one or two wee words
And drop my head and bow.

Ballyvarley Ghost.

22nd July Tuesday 2008.

It was always on a Wednesday about eight o'clock at night,
Always in the winter time which added to the fright,
There wasn't any country lights which added to the dark,
And we were waiting patiently
for the ghost to make its mark.

Then sure enough just past the hour
the silent ghost appeared,
We stood with mouths wide open
as the neighbours spoke of fear,
And not a one could understand
just where this spirit was born,
It sat so still and silent laughing down at us with scorn.

Well this was now a weekly thing more gathered on the road,
Some brought tea and sandwiches
as up and down they strode,
And they all waited patiently for some brave man to say,
That he would go and break the ice before the end of day.

But no one went, not one brave gent
the light it shone so bright,
Into the early hours we stood, away into the night,
Then suddenly it disappeared as fast as eyes could blink,
And left us all our lives enthralled to go to bed and think.

But it never made a difference next week it came and went,
No one could solve the mystery
what the light could represent,
So from then on we gathered to propose each one a toast
To drink our health and drink our wealth
To the Ballyvarley GHOST.

Flax Pulling.

23rd July Wednesday 2008.

The year was nineteen sixty two when I was only ten,
My father grew a field of flax, to be hand pulled by men,
And I was there to give a hand to help my father out,
Absorbing all was going on, what life was all about.

It was really hard hard work, your back was bent all day,
And you went home so tired at night all for so little pay,
But this was what you had to do there wasn't any choice,
You toiled away without a say and never raised your voice.

The flax was pulled with roots and all nothing went to waste,
The fibres long as possible they were raised up to your waist,
Now the beets as they were known were transported to the dam,
They retted there for fourteen days packed and neatly crammed .

Now you had to stand up to your knees in stinking water cold
Removing all those sodden beets required some self control,
For the fermentation process caused an awful noxious smell,
You dare not focus in on it or for a moment dwell.

The Lint hole banks you draped with flax and let it lie for hours
It then was grassed out on the fields to dry between the showers,
And when the sun had done its job in a dozen days or so,
The wind would finally separate, the plant from fibres blow.

Now the scutch mill it was waiting for the bundles to be sent
The workers waited patiently all familiar with the scent,
For the flax it went through breaking
and the hackling process too,
The scutchers were a vital part of making yarn for you.

The Billy Goat.

24th July Thursday 2008.

It was always so frustrating when a Billy kid was born,
My father used to do his best for us to be fore warned,
For it was just no good to him he never could afford,
Too keep this blasted Billy goat, it had to face the sword.

We could never understand we were too young back then,
But daddy said it's useless like a hen that wasn't laying,
So this we kid was for the chop Mick Trainor was the man,
To take it for his greyhounds was part of daddy's plan.

But this was not intentional, not on our Dads behalf,
So we could never blame him or write his epitaph,
For he was always looking milk, a female goat too breed,
But of responsibility from this one he was freed.

It was the biggest drawback when we were keeping goats,
For there was no way of knowing and there was no antidote,
You had to take whatever make was in the overcoat,
And hope and pray that on the day twas not a Billy goat.

But the milk was so important when we were all at home
It was used to make the porridge
and the pudding honeycombs,
So even though it was shame the Billy goats to slay,
It meant we didn't hunger and we lived another day.

And yet there was no reason why, no one was ever told
Why we never killed the kids and kept them for our bowls,
But maybe that's the way it was, you didn't kill your own
You give them to a neighbour man
to use them skin and bone.

Total Celebration.

25th July Friday 2008.

When I'm lacking inspiration
and there's nothing on my mind,
It's as if my eyes are closed - and I am going blind,
For when I look around me at all of Gods creation
There is plenty for to write about
A Total Celebration.

You listen to the birds on call their voices fill the air,
You look at all the lovely trees
they're blooming everywhere,
And when you turn your head upwards
sure the sea is upside down,
Blue and orange and colours red
and silver clouds all round,
Put them all together and its then you realise,
That human minds like ours
could never make something this size.

And yet I'm lacking inspiration and my mind is going blank,
I don't understand the reason it's as if my brain has shrank,
And when you come to think of it the truth's not hard to see,
For were paying no attention to the beauty that is free,
You see were always so consumed
with the pressures of the world,
And were waiting for the news
another episode to unfold,
Yet all around this little piece
of earth that you've been given,
There's enough to fill a thousand times
The days that you've been living.

Essential Ingredients.

26th July Saturday 2008.

A home it has ingredients
Where parents and children dwell,
And depending on their attitudes
Could be Heaven, or be Hell.

A school it has ingredients
Where teachers and pupils relate,
Skills pass on to the future
And every thing's up for debate.

A church it has ingredients
Where human families live,
With feeling at the foremost
And we all learn to forgive.

A community has ingredients
Made up of flesh and blood,
Where love is a shared experience
Tears of joy and sorrow flood.

The workplace has ingredients
the important one being respect,
Where everyone pulls together
and freedom is always direct.
For its here that we all make relations
and its here that we all make good friends,
It is here where the seeds they are sown
that our privileged society depends.

American Presidents.

27th July Sunday 2008.

There has always been a fascination I truly have to say
Concerning all the presidents of the continent USA.

George Washington took the office,
back in seventeen eighty nine
In seventeen ninety seven, John Adams drew the line.
And then came Thomas Jefferson in eighteen hundred and one
In eighteen hundred and nine there was James Madison.
James Monroe he took his office in eighteen seventeen
In eighteen twenty five Quincy Adams came on the scene.
Well Andrew Jackson took his post in eighteen twenty nine
In eighteen thirty seven Martin Van Buren was assigned.
The turn of William Harrison came in eighteen forty one
And after just a single month John Tyler jumped the gun.
Now James J Polk was president in eighteen forty five
In eighteen forty nine Zachary Taylor he arrived.
And after just a single year Millard Fillmore took his place
Replaced in eighteen fifty three by a new man, Franklin Pierce.
Then James Buchanan came along in eighteen fifty seven
And then in eighteen sixty one the famous Abraham Lincoln.
Andrew Johnson was voted in the year eighteen sixty five
In eighteen sixty nine Ulysses Grant he gained the prize.
Rutherford B Hayes was elected in eighteen seventy seven
Then in eighteen eighty one James Garfield was in heaven.
Chester Arthur he took over just a few months down the road
Then in eighteen eighty five
'twas Grover Cleveland's new abode.
Benjamin Harrison got promoted in eighteen eighty nine
In eighteen ninety three Grover Cleveland back in line.
William Mc Kinley he took over in eighteen ninety seven
Nineteen hundred and one Theodore Roosevelt up in heaven.

American Presidents (continued).

William Taft was 27ᵗʰ in nineteen hundred and nine
Then in nineteen thirteen Woodrow Wilson was in line.
Well Warren G Harding came in nineteen twenty one
 Nineteen twenty three Calvin Coolidge made the run.
Herbert Hoover got his turn in nineteen twenty nine
 In nineteen thirty three Franklin Roosevelt he was fine.
Harry Truman came along then in nineteen forty five
And in nineteen fifty three Dwight Eisenhower came alive.
John F Kennedy came on board then in nineteen sixty one
Two years later Lyndon Johnson, and his work was begun.
Richard Nixon was the next man in nineteen sixty nine
Nineteen seventy four saw Gerald Ford proclaim it's mine.
Jimmy Carter was elected then in nineteen seventy seven
Nineteen eighty one Ronald Reagan on cloud eleven.
George W Bush succeeded him in nineteen eighty nine
Nineteen ninety three and Bill Clinton was to shine.
The Democrats were ousted then in the year 2001
A new man in the white house and it was George's son.
To keep it in the family his name George W Bush
And he'll be going nowhere he's not in any rush.
But his term is running out now eight years is nearly done
Will McCain land on the bright side,
Or will Obama bring the sun?

A Man's Gotta Do.

29th July Tuesday 2008.

A man's gotta do what a man's gotta do,
He has to live his life and see it through,
He should not be lead by the leader of the pack
But for his own beliefs go to hell and back.

A man should not put all his faith in men,
But rather look at his life every now and then,
And when he looks at himself and all his mistakes,
Remember that a man needs to kill his own snakes.

For there comes a time he has to stand firm,
An experience we all, should stop and learn,
It's part of the peace in your life that's found,
When you firmly keep your feet on the ground.

So he lives his life and wants to settle down,
Have a wee house on a nice piece of ground,
Remember if he wants to see the setting sun
An east coast house won't be much fun.

This journey it's short no matter how long,
Life has to be lived for the weak and the strong,
So don't be afraid as you live each day,
And make some decisions along the way.

A Man's Gotta Do it.

Family Ties.

30ᵗʰ July Wednesday 2008.

Keep in touch with all your family
as your life progresses through,
Do not lose sight of their presence
Remember, they have got lives too.

Firstly take your sons and daughters
they're the closest to your heart,
Let them know that you still love them
as they make their own fresh start.

Don't forget your aunts and uncles
and your cousins one and all
Take the time for your dear Grandma
give your Granda a wee call.

For your family are important
and they are your flesh and blood,
Do not let your knowledge of them
get washed away in life's great flood.

Retirement Hopes.

31ˢᵗ July Thursday 2008.

Can I afford to look ahead to the age of 65,
Sure I can only take for granted
I might be still alive,
Why I'm rushing it would seem
To hurry through my life,
I can't wait to get the pension
me and her, you know, the wife.

Can I afford not to listen
To the men with all the brains
Telling me to move in closer
to all the faster lanes,
Put in more and more good money
pack in more to your oul bag,
And then when you retire
life won't be one long oul drag.

But can I afford to work much harder
will my body take the strain,
And even if I do, how much more
do I stand to gain,
For even if the future
and the money might be right,
I could be pushing up the daises
A long way out of sight.

August

Titles of Poems	*Month of August*		
The Headless Man	1st August	Friday	2008
Set In Your Ways	2nd August	Saturday	2008
God Laughs Too	3rd August	Sunday	2008
The Colosseum	4th August	Monday	2008
How???	5th August	Tuesday	2008
Call of Nature	6th August	Wednesday	2008
Brain Cells	7th August	Thursday	2008
Balderdash	8th August	Friday	2008
The Busy Man	9th August	Saturday	2008
Days of Yore	10th August	Sunday	2008
The Final Journey	11th August	Monday	2008
The Invitation	12th August	Tuesday	2008
" Words"	13th August	Wednesday	2008
Insomnia	14th August	Thursday	2008
Welcome Home Dad	15th August	Friday	2008
Ronnie Drew	16th August	Saturday	2008
Matrimony	17th August	Sunday	2008
Shared Love	18th August	Monday	2008
Nice New Car	19th August	Tuesday	2008
Tale Of Tails	20th August	Wednesday	2008
It's In The Genes	21st August	Thursday	2008
Omagh	22ndAugust	Friday	2008
The Alphabet	23rd August	Saturday	2008

Family Day Out	24th August	Sunday	2008
Twice A Child	25th August	Monday	2008
Globing Warming ??	26th August	Tuesday	2008
My Birthday	27th August	Wednesday	2008
Breaking Up	28th August	Thursday	2008
False Teeth	29th August	Friday	2008
Pills Or Bills!	30th August	Saturday	2008
This Wee Job	31st August	Sunday	2008

Headless Man.

1ˢᵗ August Friday 2008.

I will tell you all a story about a man who had no head
And every day he wakened up he thought that he was dead,
But even though his body wanted to remain in bed
He got up and washed himself and went to Mass instead.

Well sitting in the Chapel, up beside the Altar near
The Priest he spoke of God, and love and sin and truth and fear,
But because this man up sitting there, he didn't have no ears
It never made a difference because he couldn't hear.

Now some of the parishioners, mostly women I presume,
They tidy up the Chapel every Saturday afternoon,
And although the place was spotless,
free from spiders webs and flies
It didn't have an impact because this man he had no eyes.

Well he sat beside the window cill a bowl was full of flowers
Their fragrance filled the Chapel air,
the scent was overpowering,
But even though he sat throughout, for quite a lengthy spell
He was spiked with unawareness for he had no sense of smell.

Now right beside him in the seat this single mother sat
Her husband he had left her for a blondie blue eyed brat,
But when a tear fell from her eye a friendly word she spoke
His body fell in silence, this shaken headless bloke.

He couldn't even touch someone to lend a helping hand
Because he had no senses then he could not understand,
So stop for just a moment and the line of truth pursue
When it comes to my wee poem
Could this headless man be you?

Set In Your Ways.

2nd August Saturday 2008.

You can lead a horse to the water
but you cannot make him drink,
Study this old saying and it will really make you think,
Just what exactly does it mean you have to be aware
So I will try to analyze the meaning I declare.

Now put it in perspective, I will not lead you astray
It is not so very difficult if you listen to what I say,
But that is just the problem when it comes to my advice
If you're not prepared to listen
You can thirst to be precise.

There is no use in being forceful
for it simply does not work,
Just be gently persuasive or
you'll drive yourself berserk,
For when it comes to action
It's of personal concern,
As to whether those responsible
are prepared to take their turn.

For sometimes you can burst yourself
to change another's ways,
And even to convince yourself
that there'll be better days,
But when the pressure's on you
To produce the goods – just think,
'You can lead a horse to water
But you cannot make him drink'.

God Laughs Too.

3rd August Sunday 2008.

Sometimes I get sick of praying
As if it's a waste of time,
So I just stop and say no more
It's there I draw the line,

Then I take the time and plan my day
And tell God what I'll do,
I try to smile and have a laugh
And I hear God laughing too.

The dawn leads on too quick to noon
And soon it passes three,
It's not too long before I know
That he's laughing straight at me.

But I am so preoccupied
With doing my own thing,
I carry on regardless
With my going nowhere fling.

For God has seen it all before
He lets me have my way,
He knows that I'll be back to him
Before the end of day.

The Colosseum.

4th August Monday 2008.

I watched a programme lately
away back in Roman times,
It resembled Duffy's Circus, it was like a pantomime,
The only thing about it was the lions were being fed
with living human beings
all around the death walls spread.

Well these people they were young and old
and male and female too,
They were treated worse than animals
Just to feed a barbecue,
And you never could imagine
in all your wildest dreams,
How this wicked man Tiberius
could be driven to such extremes.

Now I know it was a programme
just portraying days of old,
But it was a true reflection
of those innocent guiltless souls,
They were in the colosseum to fulfil spectators' greed
to satisfy and entertain their selfish bloody needs.

And when you sit and think
of all that happened in the past
Those days of Roman butchery
to the harmless working class,
For this barbaric act of inhumanity to man,
never could be justified and always should be dammed.

How ???

5th August Tuesday 2008.

How do you stop time from passing they say
Do you take all the clocks and throw them away,
How do you freeze the years that decay
do you put them on ice,
and hope that they stay.
What do you do when your hair starts to stray
Or changes its colour from ginger to grey,
How do you change the way people age
Do you turn the book back page after page,
How do we alter the way that we look
or take back the youth
the years have just took.
How do you turn off the pains that you feel
as your body gets older
from head down to heel,
How do you mind all the things your Ma said,
Do you stop watching TV
and read more instead.
How do you stop all the things in your head
From turning to dust before you are dead,
Well from writing this poem
I have come to believe,
That dwelling on life could turn you to grieve
So take a deep breath and don't feel so dull,
It's the candle that's withered
That has lived to the full.

Call of Nature.

6th August. Wednesday. 2008.

There was an old fellow laying in his hospital bed
I can't remember who,
But he rang the bell to call the nurse
To take him to the loo,
Now he was so impatient but nature had its call,
He was afraid to go himself in case that he would fall.

Well eventually the nurse appeared,
she said "who rang the bell?"
Says he "the culprit laying here and I'm feeling so unwell,
But if I don't get to that wee door
that shows the sign for men,
You'll be going for the bucket and a mop for me again".

"Well don't you dare", she said to him,
"Or trouble you'll be in,
I'll go and get a bottle you can fill it to the brim",
But he was so insistent that he would walk the floor
"You can keep your little bottle and take me to that door".

The nurse by now was angry and she urged him to remain,
"Now you just pull your horns in boy
Get back to bed again,
Just take this plastic bottle and relieve yourself right now
For I am loosing patience if you're looking for a row".

So Paddy Joe conceded all and crept back into bed
He took her little bottle and he peed in it instead,
She turned to him with a smirky grin
and asked "why all the dread?"
"What I am thinking now, my dear,
Would be better left unsaid"

Brain Cells.

7th August Thursday 2008.

It is a well known proven fact that everyone has a brain,
Why some are better than others
would be difficult to explain,
But listening to the experts, the ones who study science,
it would seem the whole thing functions
like an electrical appliance.

Now it used to be conclusive that the brain was all in one,
And intelligence it flowed from what went in
and what you done,
But it seems for many years now
and there's evidence to prove,
That the human brain is split in two
and is simple to improve.

So imagine it's a melon and you chop it clean in two,
The left side it is different, has an opposite point of view,
It is not that there is conflict with the side that's on the right,
But there's different information to wet your appetite.

For it would seem the left is negative
full of worry, fear and dread,
And in times of awful crisis it is hard to clear your head,
For it always sees the dark side that says there's no way out,
Full of fright and apprehension, and always full of doubt.

But according to the experts who have studied this great cell
The right side lies more dormant but is craving to rebel,
For everything is positive and could turn your life around,
If you could find the secret the results could be profound.

Balderdash.

8th August Friday 2008.

'Fools and their money are easy parted',
My father used to say,
Some typical examples, sure we see them every day,
For many people con themselves deposits on the line,
And end up totally broken their lives in steep decline.

The one thing to hit the top
over this last few years
has been the slump in property,
leaving many folks in tears,
Especially on the continent
where things have fell apart,
and some greedy developers
operate without a heart.

Now many people on in years
set out to buy their dreams,
The lure of Spanish properties
would change their lives supreme,
But many they were foolish and were only lead astray,
the return for them was misery,
Painful memories every day.

So it's always worth considering,
when a magnet sucks you in,
If some of these great offers are really genuine,
So if indeed you feel the need
to spend your hard earned cash,
Is it really worth the hassle
or just simply Balderdash?

The Busy Man.

9th August Saturday 2008.

He was not renowned for working
This wee man he was scared stiff,
But a message in his letterbox said
That he would have to shift,
For he'd been on the bru' now for as long as he could mind,
He said that they were good to him
And that they were awful kind.

But the good days they are over
And all things are going to change,
Though this would be impossible
For himself to rearrange,
For it has been so long now and his life is well planned out,
In fact he is so busy
Going around and knocking about.

But it hardly matters anyway
for his youth has passed him by,
There's not much hope of him sweating now
Or trying to diversify,
For there simply is no likelihood
of his payments being withdrawn,
And there certainly is no hope of him
a sitting down to mourn.

So he gathered up his message which intended him to work,
And he took it to the station where he said,
"The policemen lurk",
He proclaimed " I'm pressing charges
On a personal vendetta,
For in the post today,
I have received 'A Threatening Letter'!"

Days of Yore.

10th August Sunday 2008.

They all got into a circle and stories they were told
All mostly of the bad times and in the days of old,
When they had to walk across the fields
Carry water from the well
And live in old mud houses,
where their ancestors used to dwell.

Now some would chew tobacco
and some would smoke a fag,
And some would even pass one round
and give his mate a drag,
But the craic was mostly good
and you could listen to their laments,
A lullaby of days gone by and yet no discontent.

For they mostly all were happy
even though the times were hard,
And it seemed to make a difference
Just to share with some regard,
Now each one took his turn to speak
And tell his urgent tale,
Without an interruption from the company they inhaled.

Well none of them were burdened
with the luxuries we have now,
And the only thing they had to leave
was their two hands on the plough,
So living out the past for them was not a time to moan,
For it just reversed the future
which for them was all unknown.

The Final Journey.

11th August Monday 2008.

Darling… I'm on my way to heaven
It's a journey I have to make,
I am hoping to meet my Saviour
and for him my soul to take.

Do not be too concerned for me
I'm not travelling on my own,
A group of friends are meeting me
to see Jesus on his throne.

Try not to shed too many tears
that will only cause you grief,
Just focus on the great years spent
It will bring you some relief.

For one of us will have to leave
the other there's no cure,
And when we do the parting
won't be easy that's for sure.

But crying for me when I'm dead my dear
Won't do no good at all,
Just remember me as the one you loved
And someday I'll return your call.

The Invitation.

12th August Tuesday 2008.

Rawden was a rich man but felt very insecure,
Regarding who his friends were, he was never very sure,
They were always hanging round him
and appeared some every day,
But they never seemed that interested in what he had to say.

So he organised a party and invited one and all,
To his mansion on the hillside he called them to a ball,
And when they all arrived in style, he led them down below,
down to the deepest dungeon, a hundred of them, or so.

He sat them down on cold, hard chairs,
at a table old and bleak,
And served them up with porridge
It was tasteless, thin and weak,
And very soon excuses flowed, the exodus begun,
In less than thirty minutes they were reduced to twenty one.

Well, Rawden now he stood and said,
"My friends come follow me"
He took them up the darkest stairs and across the balcony,
He opened up the finest doors that lead to this grand hall,
Where greeted them magnificence,
with servants at their call.

Now Rawden once again he stood
And addressed them all "My friends"
I invite you all to take your seats and we will start again,
For now I know for certain, and I don't feel insecure,
For knowing who my friends are,
In the future I'll be sure.

"Words".

13th August Wednesday 2008.

Sometimes when I listen
to all that's going on,
I feel so disillusioned
trying to write this song,
For it seems there's nothing positive
to put in words right now,
So I'll wait until tomorrow
then I will not have to lie.

And when tomorrow comes around
no changes can be found,
Out of the mouths of all the News
It's just the same old sound,
I'll try to wait another day
and hope for better things,
To cover up the failings
of those who pull the strings.

And when another week has passed
And all remains the same
I'll try to get my head around
the things I do again,
Sometime I will listen
To all that's going on,
And I will write them on this paper
And try to make a song.

Insomnia.

14th August Thursday 2008.

It's a long, long night when you can't sleep tight
and you're restless in your bed,
When you twist and turn and your eye lids burn
and you're laying awake instead.

It's a wearisome night when that clock strikes
and you haven't shut an eye,
When the moon and stars disappear from afar
and the night has passed you by.

And you lie on your back and you lie on your side
First the left one then the right,
Then you take to the floor
and you head for the door
of the fridge for a drink of sprite.

Then bleary eyed back to bed you decide
which position to take up next,
Do you lie on your belly or go and watch telly
Waste an hour with the tele text.

But it's not very pleasant when you cannot sleep
It's a hell of a long - long night,
I've been there now so I know for myself
Exactly what it is like,
And it makes so little difference
What you do or do not do,
If you cannot sleep you cannot sleep
It's too bad for you know who.

Welcome Home Dad.

15th August Friday 2008.

I can always remember back in years
my daddy coming home,
He always wore a pair of boots
his socks were darned and sewn,
He worked up on the motorway a new road was being built,
The men all worked together
to lay a brand new tarmac quilt,
Now it was never easy and the days were very long,
he carried his wee lunch box
laboured long hours for a song.

And nearly every evening when he stepped out of the van,
We were waiting there to greet him
 and to take him by the hand,
Now his lunch was bread and butter
with no ham or salad cream,
But complaints were not his making
and he lived with little dreams,
And in some ways we're all caught up
 in this life of sheer routine,
With no escape from all red tape
two rocks and your in between.

But going back to daddy to that box he had for lunch,
He always kept a sandwich for one of us to munch,
And I am sure now looking back to all those years ago,
There were times he could have eaten it upon himself bestow,
But he treated us that small amount a new mouth every day
The lessons that he taught in it, to share will always stay.

59

Ronnie Drew.

16th August Saturday 2008.

I want to pay a tribute to a singer we all knew,
He had the finest voice of all
his name is Ronnie Drew,
Renowned for singing ballads
and his diction was superb,
You could hear his words so clearly
every noun and every verb.

Well he was a bearded singer
so distinctive was his looks,
He formed his group The Dubliners
and his life would fill ten books,
Now he teamed with musicians
they were fine beyond compare,
They travelled all across the world
such talents they were rare.

But Ronnie he was so unique
his voice was deep and pure,
He focused on the story every song it went on tour,
For he had such a talent to relate to you in words,
You instantly were filled with awe
at everything you heard.

Now it was sad to see him, without his familiar beard,
To watch an icon figure in good health we all preferred,
But time had caught up with him
and his cancer was advanced,
The world was soon to loose him
but our spirits he enhanced.

Matrimony.

17th August Sunday 2008.

Getting married years ago was not a big affair,
There was no spending fortunes
wedding dresses, perming hairs,
You met up in the morning
and said yes to tie the knot,
And everybody then went home
and the whole thing was forgot.

Now the man he made a promise
to take on this brand new wife,
To take her home to cook and sew
and brush up his new life,
And when it came to honeymoons
the meadow was the choice
To cut the grass and mow the hay
And never raise your voice.

Well I'm not talking centuries
that all this was the norm,
Back in the nineteen thirties
marriage happened close to dawn,
And there was an explanation
for this early union bond,
the day would not be wasted
if you happened to abscond.

But to take the whole thing serious
and ponder on the day
It simply was a signature on a document to say,
That you and her got married
and it was all legal now,
So just get on with loving
And living out your vows.

Shared Love.

18th August Monday 2008.

Tell me what I'm like when I am near you
Fill my heart with sunshine if you will,
Satisfy my yearnings and desires too
Feelings of this kind cannot stand still.

Nothing on this earth can equal your love
Always in abundance you can give,
Sharing is no problem for my winged dove,
Giving me the breath I need to live.

Explaining it for me is not an option
There are no words to make it sound so true,
It's just a built in simple wee reaction
And a gift that God has given to so few.

You don't ask me to return your sense of longing
You don't expect to hear me say I thank you dear,
There's no pressure on me now to try responding
But I deeply need to feel your body near.

So some day when I grow older and much wiser
I will understand the beauty of your ways,
Throughout my life you've been my stabilizer
In return you've never asked me to repay.

Nothing on this earth can equal your love
Always in abundance you can give,
Sharing is no problem for my winged love
Giving me the breath I need to live.

Nice New Car.

19th August Tuesday 2008.

I met my neighbour recently
they had bought a brand new car,
And I simply was not thinking
When they waved like film stars,
Well I thought now who could that be
as I travelled on at speed,
But I could not put together, who it was I did concede,
And as I proceeded onwards on my journey that fine day,
I could see these perfect strangers,
behind the windscreen going away.

It was really so annoying and I could not comprehend,
Who it was I met on that short stretch
nearly drove me round the bend,
I knew I did not recognize the car when it appeared
With flashing lights and waving arms
The faces were not clear,
So I tried to shift the misery to the back side of my brain
And I never fully realised, how something could remain.

In the name of God who could they be
in that big flashy car,
But all to no avail for me
Who were these film stars,
So I returned to base that day
informed my wife first thing,
She said your lovely daughter
and her husband had a fling,
It was so very sudden and temptation won the day
But when the payment book arrives
They may not be so gay.

Tale of Tails.

20th August Wednesday 2008.

There are things I can remember when I was just a lad,
That happened in the countryside
you could say that this was mad,
For I was maybe ten back then this story I will cram,
On going to help my uncle Dan
to take the tails off lambs.

We packed them in a small wee barn
we each one had a job,
Disinfectant spray I had to use
when the lamb began to sob,
Now Dan held them from struggling
and John he made the cut,
And very soon the lamb let loose
with a wee small bleeding butt.

Each time a tail was severed
away from its woolly fleece,
John raised his arm in silence
and the tail he would release,
Out through an open window
a pile of them now lay,
My face was red with moisture
I was indisposed that day.

Now Dan he pushed round counting
to see which lamb was skipped,
Whilst I had scrambled out the door
afraid I would be sick,

I counted up the tails that lay
and shouted through the wall,
How many heads have you in there
He bellowed fifty four and all,
I lay there on the ground that day
my head was spinning round,
Then shouted with excitement
That's how many tails I've found.

It's In the Genes.

21ˢᵗ August Thursday 2008.

There is nothing you could do in life
That would make you feel so good,
Than looking up your family tree
Well just everybody should.

To get back to your great grandparents
Then you are doing very well,
And from all this information
There's a lot that you can tell.

For the genes that's in our children
They are not all ours alone,
But they go back generations
And they all make up a home.

So if you are not familiar
With all the family you belong,
Then make the time and effort
And confront it all head on.

Now the facts that you'll discover
Will surprise you all the way,
Why your offspring is a lawyer
Or involved in cabaret.

So I urge you all to take the time
And poke back through your dust
And when you do you'll realize

A family tree is just a must.

Omagh.

22nd August Friday 2008.

Everybody's haunted of events ten years ago,
Twas then a bomb in Omagh left a devastating blow,
For with out a single warning it wrecked this quiet town,
And killed so many people it was like a battle ground,

For suddenly the quiet of that busy shopping place,
Was rapidly disrupted by this massive dark embrace,
And in ten or fifteen seconds there was carnage everywhere,
Dust and dirt and stones and mortar
Scattered on the thoroughfare.

Now it seemed for just a moment that all hell had shed its doors,
There were yells of screaming terror as in scenes of any war,
And confusion was the setting as the air began to clear,
The extent of all the damage was beginning to appear.

There were bodies on the footpaths
there were bodies on the street,
There were cries of sheer commotion intermingled in retreat,
For the people they were running to escape the tangled mess,
For those of us not there that day our minds could only guess.

Well since that day in August in nineteen ninety eight
The relatives of victims they have sought to captivate,
The minds of politicians and of Law and Order too,
To try to bring to justice, which is long since overdue.

But it seems the weeds will always grow
among the autumn corn,
For charging those responsible may have to be with drawn,
But eventually the time will come and it will be too late,
For those who carried out this crime they will not Negotiate.

The Alphabet.

23rd August Saturday 2008.

The alphabet it has letters made up of twenty six
It's a truly and amazing wonderful box of tricks,
For jumble all the letters up and you will make a word
Form them then together and a sentence will be heard.

For A is for Accordion, acoustics and accord,
B is for the brains behind the backstage boys on board,
C controls the candidates that celebrate the charts,
D is for diversity, democracy and departs.

E is everlasting, emphasizing everything
F is for foundation, fundamental, fox and fling,
G it guards the glamorous the glitter and the gold
H is for the highwayman, hypocrisy and hold.

I is illustrating, instrumental, inhumane,
J is just for Jonathan for Jason and for Jane.
K it kills the kindness of a kinder garden kid
L is legislative, legalising ladies lib.

M maintains its movements, mostly meaningfull
N needs nothing nowadays, nice, neat and natural,
O opens opportunities and officially overflows
P paints a pretty picture, parties, paths and patios.

Now Q and R and S and T are important letters too
If you want words to suit them I'll leave it up to U,
'Cause I'm V ery V ery W eary as X finds me at Y
Z is zooming Zealous, "So, you give it a try".

Family Day Out.

24ᵗʰ August Sunday 2008.

One day I was walking twas in the spring time
I heard the train calling going through Scarva line,
The years in my memory began to unwind
The day that train left us all sitting behind.

For we were all young when this shock came our way
We had all walked to Scarva on that lovely spring day,
And we stood at the station excitement was high
Just waiting to board that big steel dragon fly.

Now sessions like this they were mostly so rare
For getting to Warrenpoint was an expensive affair,
But this was a luxury our mother had planned
To go on a day trip to a far away land.

Well we headed through Acton and up to Jerrettspass
When the brakes on the train slowed
the wheels down from fast,
And soon we were waiting all bored on the line,
we were told by the driver that all would be fine.

It seemed that another train met us that day
It was coming from Newry, Gorrawood the main stay,
But we were the nearest to Scarva it seemed
We had to reverse back and gone were our dreams.

And as the train sat there with time running out
We could hear porters shouting and buzzing about,
It would have to go backwards to the end of the line
In Scarva train station we were all left behind.

Twice A Child.

Old age it is inevitable if you live long enough,
And for some it's not a problem
they are made of powerful stuff,
They go on and on for ever it would seem to you and me,
Always full of energy
they're as happy as can be.

Now that is such a blessing
for the ones that don't grow old,
They fill their lives with outings
and they give a hundred fold,
Now for those who take an illness
when the twilight years unpack,
It can be prolonged for ever
whilst some don't last a crack.

For those whose lives have ended
at an age say eighty three,
Then "they had a good oul innings"
And they lived abundantly,
But for those whose lives have ended
And remain in stately care,
It's a difficult situation and for them sometimes despair.

For the years they rob your beauty
And your youth has slipped away,
There's people now around you
You're being cared for every day,
It certainly reminds you seeing someone meek and mild
Of a very common saying -
"Once a man and twice a child".

Global Warming??

26th August Tuesday 2008.

The rains they are unusual, the floods are just the same
I never do remember, in all my life such rain,
There seems to be no stop to it, where does it all end up
For when it lies a day or two, you never see a sup.

But go to bed at night time and waken up again
And you will find throughout the night
another slap of rain,
And that's been going on now for nearly all the year
We didn't have a summer time, but a winter atmosphere.

You listen to the experts
when they talk of climate change
Believing them is difficult, but it's certainly very strange,
For I remember years ago we had this endless sun
You could have planned at any time
To have yourself some fun.

But nowadays its different, you simply cannot plan
You wait until the morning till you hear the weatherman,
And then you try to organize your daily work routine
It all revolves around the sun
and the showers that's in between.

But try hard not to grumble
for we cannot change the weather,
Even though you may be near the end of that long tether
Just try to go along with it and strive to ride the storm,
If climate change means more, more rain
then rain will be the norm.

My Birthday.

27th August Wednesday 2008.

Today I have a birthday
I am fifty six years old,
And in case you had forgotten
Don't say you've not been told,
But to wish me "Happy Birthday"
Is the last thing on my mind.
So I hope you're not offended
If I seem to be unkind.

For as each year progresses
To the ones that I have left,
It's another year that's closer
To the one that stops your breath,
But it always is a treasure
Just to reach this time of life,
Because every day's a bonus
With joy mixed up with strife.

So it's not that I'm ungrateful
And I thank you for your cards,
But I will not be disgruntled
If you've been caught off guard,
It is different when you're younger
For it's a chance to celebrate,
Please forgive at this moment
I'd just leave forget this date.

Breaking Up.

28th August Thursday 2008.

Don't you tell me you don't love me
for I don't want to know,
If you decide it's over, then just get up and go
But do not cause me any pain that I could never bear,
Just think it over carefully
don't leave my heart to tear.

I can't understand the reasons
or what brought this all about,
Your loyalty and love for me, has never been in doubt
But now I have to ask myself was I a fool for love
and have I just allowed it all to come down from above.

For everybody makes mistakes and I can understand
but this just makes no sense to me
I'm left in no mans land,
So take another look before there is no turning back
and hopefully we can change the coarse
and get back on the track.

But if it doesn't happen and you cannot change your mind
then I'll have to just accept the fact - another path to find,
But this will not be easy for I'm permanently in shock
for down the years of joy and tears
You've always been my rock.

So once again I say to you don't shed your love for me
don't even think of leaving I am making you a plea,
Just let us take a long hard look
at where we both went wrong
and put the whole thing in the past
in the words of this wee song.

False Teeth.

I laugh at my grandchildren when they ask to see my teeth
For their eyes roll in amazement and in total disbelief,
They don't expect to see my teeth there sitting in my hand
As if like some magician
I had waved a magic wand.

And then I put them in again and try to keep them hid
And they can't understand, how I had did what I had did,
But I will wind them up and say my teeth are like the stars
I tell them they come out at night,
I keep them in a jar.

But they will shout out loud at me to try to see my teeth,
They even try to pull them with their fingers from beneath,
But I just hold on firmly saying they are all my own
Though it's hard to fool the youngsters
Who say, "Granda yours have flown"

So we just mess around a bit and they make fun of me
It's very hard for them to know exactly what they see,
But very soon they all get tired and come to understand
That while they're trying to get their teeth
Mine are in my hand.

"When we are old like you Granda,
  will all our teeth fall out?"
"Is this what mummy tells us, eating sweets is all about?"
So I don't try to change the notions all of them possess
I tell them, cleaning them each day is the secret of success.

Pills Or Bills!

30th August Saturday 2008.

When I was wakening every day
to the postman bringing bills
I couldn't have foreseen the time
I'd be swapping them for pills,
But back in June a month or two
this came to pass my way
An operation meant for me eating tablets every day.

I got four every morning and four of them at noon
At six o'clock and evening time it all came round too soon,
And most of them they were for pain
Just to keep me from being sore
At times it was so bad for me
I had to ask for more.

Well ever since the month of June I've had to eat my pills
Right now I'd give a fortune just to swap them for my bills
For we take so much for granted
getting up to face each day,
To be thankful for our blessings
and being in good health to pay.

But thank God for me they're easing
and I'm down to four a day
The pain that I was always in
has almost gone away,
And so I'm looking forward to
when the bills drop in the post,
I know to have a choice for me
Which I'll be choosing most!

This Wee Job.

31ˢᵗ August Sunday 2008.

If you have a job that you're needing done
You know, one that's been laying around,
Then this can become a wee job of its own
For usually, no one can be found.

You see people today are all backward
When it comes to take on the wee chores,
They're afraid 'twill upset all their benefits,
Jeopardise all the oaths that they swore.

They used to be tempted with pound notes
For an hour or two's work every day,
But now they refuse to be cornered
And they'll tell you it just doesn't pay.

Now insurance is always an issue
If you're looking a young lad to weed,
Most likely you'll break some commandants
And be stopped before you proceed.

So you ring on the phone the professionals
And you get them too give you a price
You'll need the bank to give you a mortgage
And a solicitor to get some advice.

So you stop and appoint the long finger
For three fortunes you can't take on board,
This wee job it is just so enormous
You simply just cannot afford.

September

Titles Of Poems	*Month Of September*		
Ambitions	1st September	Monday	2008
Moving On	2nd September	Tuesday	2008
Ice Cubes	3rd September	Wednesday	2008
Talents	4th September	Thursday	2008
On A Mission	5th September	Friday	2008
Judge Not	6th September	Saturday	2008
Frustration	7th September	Sunday	2008
What's Your Name?	8th September	Monday	2008
A Prayer	9th September	Tuesday	2008
Unexplored Territory	10th September	Wednesday	2008
One For Sorrow	11th September	Thursday	2008
Teamwork	12th September	Friday	2008
Puzzled	13th September	Saturday	2008
The Dentist's Chair	14th September	Sunday	2008
Contentment	15th September	Monday	2008
Lesson Inhaled	16th September	Tuesday	2008
The Visiting	17th September	Wednesday	2008
Secret Love	18th September	Thursday	2008
Nonsense/Cycle of Life	19th September	Friday	2008
Time Doesn't Wait	20th September	Saturday	2008
In The Final	21st September	Sunday	2008
Unrepeatable	22ndSeptember	Monday	2008
Human Kindness	23rd September	Tuesday	2008

Colum	24th September	Wednesday	2008
Delivery Suite	25th September	Thursday	2008
Problems On Board	26th September	Friday	2008
Abortion	27th September	Saturday	2008
Just Not To Be	28th September	Sunday	2008
Silver Lining	29th September	Monday	2008
Tick Tock	30th September	Tuesday	2008

Ambitions.

1st September Monday 2008.

John has opened up his site, he's going to start and build,
A goal that he has set himself, his ambition to fulfil.
His site's in Terryhoogan
just down the Scarva Road,
He set a mobile home on it, a humble wee abode,
And Anne and him are happy there,
they are comfortable and warm,
But building is their dream come true,
the whole place to transform.

And so today they made a start
the digger man appeared,
This caterpillar track machine, the site he had to clear,
He pushed the soil into a pile, and dug down to the clay,
Then levelled loads of four inch stone
to make a nice driveway.

The shuck down at the bottom,
well it needed to be piped,
But in a half a day or so, now this wee job was wiped,
And so to marking out the site, foundations to be laid
The heavy lorries on their way
the concrete ready made.

And so by Thursday morning, the first phase was prepared
It's only just a stepping stone,
no use in being scared,
But in another month or two some more work will be done
So I'll write another poem
to record for everyone.

Moving on.

2nd *September Tuesday 2008.*

I have seen many changes
down the years that have passed,
And have always been part of that
great working class,
But to live out the lives that our ancestors endured
We would not be prepared so we strived to ensure
That the future would leave us with efforts explored
Our hands and our brains we would reap the rewards.

For things were so dull our forefathers would bear
There wasn't a penny to spend on repairs,
So everything sat with a roof made of thatch
Mud walls for a building and a door with a latch,
And so they decided to just sit it out
It was far more important to live life devout.

But back in the sixties the whole thing took a turn
When a new generation were willing to learn,
So with pure dedication and a fire in our hearts
The world started changing the old ways depart,
We made big decisions to let the past go
And look to the future and improve the whole show.

Now for all the improvements some people would say
Do we live any better are we happier today?
The answer is "yes" we certainly are
The old days are in bed asleep with the stars.

Ice Cubes.

3rd September Wednesday 2008.

They sat there in the freezer as cold as cold as ice
They sat in plastic boxes in a little cube device,
There was little for to talk about the day was very long
waiting for the weekend and the merry evening songs.

Now their job was so important
when the alcohol it flowed,
They greeted dipping fingers just from every so and so,
And then to be insulted with a duty to perform
To water down a whisky to be deformed in chloroform.

But an ice cube's not important the ingredient it is cheap,
It's not something that we think of
In the freezer where they sleep,
And for me it was no different till I was forced to spend
A period in hospital when ice cubes helped me to mend.

For a week I had no water to allow my wounds to heal
They rubbed my lips with ice cubes
But I had to keep them sealed,
I can still remember as my tongue filled up my mouth,
These soothing little ice cubes
cooled my lips as I lay drowsed.

So the next time you drink vodka
or whiskey on the rocks
Just remember that wee ice cube
before your head is blocked,
For although it cost you nothing it has value way beyond
all the spirits in Ireland
and the weekend evening songs.

Talents.

4th September Thursday 2008.

Could you imagine for a moment
what the whole world would be like,
If there was no one to concern themselves
with trying to get things right,
If each one took the attitude, to simply pass the buck,
and push it on to some poor soul
and leave it all to luck.

If everyone was careless in their duties to perform,
If no one made the effort
to try and calm the storm,
Just think of all the chaos there would be in every land,
If every human person was to fail to understand.

You see, in every single act
that happens every single day,
It all involves good people who are willing to display,
The kinds of acts, and arts and facts
and talents of all kind,
That keeps the world revolving,
keeps this planet earth refined.

So if your job is being a doctor, or one who empties bins,
Then strive to do it better and be truly genuine,
If in life you have a talent
that you know could help someone,
Then for God's sake go and use it
from this moment " Life's Begun".

On A Mission.

We got on board an Aer Lingus plane it was July 2006,
and we headed off to Boston both hands on a crucifix,
For flying was not my strongest link but the technology I admire
And to get myself to Norwich was in fact my hearts desire.

For we were on a mission "Family Tree" was in my mind
The ones that left old Ireland's shores I truly had to find,
And to think in 1869 when fare wells they were bade
When Fullertons parted company
with their parents in Lisnagade.

Now in this wee piece of writing I will concentrate on Anne
She married to John Craney he was a neighbour man,
Well they went with their two children
to cross the Atlantic waves,
And they settled up in Norwich
three thousand miles they braved.

Well they both had nine more children
For big families were the norm,
There was twenty years of difference
from the first to last was born,
And we found all our relations in the archives over there
It was all recorded perfectly and diligently with care.

But I could not believe the day in all my wildest dreams
For me to meet relations in the flesh was too extreme,
His name was JR Craney his Grandmother my Great Aunt
The Anne who left in '69 her family there to plant.

And when he came to visit us at the age of seventy two,
He'd never been to Ireland for him a dream come true,
Now it was so exciting and was very worthwhile too
So my advice is check it out, it will be the same for you.

Judge Not.

6ᵗʰ September Saturday 2008.

What will the neighbours think, days are over
For people now really don't care,
It used to be skeletons only appeared
To the least well off in the square.

But times have changed who could have guessed
When no one points a finger,
When you have got some kids of your own
Your accusations linger.

For when some one had a drinking son
Who came home and mouthed out labour,
His parents always cautioned him
To think about the neighbours.

And if a girl got pregnant fell foul to decent ways,
Then the whole damn world was watching
She wasn't worth the light of day,
And shacking up together as in the present time
Well, it simply wasn't heard of,
It would have been a terrible crime.

But every thing is different now no-one escapes the net
Rich and poor are equal
when it comes to breaking sweat,
So you simply keep your mouth shut
and try to do your best
For you could be in trouble just like all the rest.

Frustration.

7th September Sunday 2008.

I am trying to cope with frustration
With not being able to work,
I'm defying my natural instincts
The satisfaction I get from the perks.

It's the first time I can remember
That I am restrained to the house,
I feel I have nothing to offer
Sitting here every day like a mouse.

Now I know every day I get stronger
And I'm feeling much better for sure,
But I am still a long way from recovery
And my patience is naturally poor.

I will have to abandon all actions
And content myself sitting about,
To allow the whole process of healing
Makes sense and removes any doubt.

So I will have to resist the temptation
And observe what the doctors have said,
There's no use trying to make an agenda
That will leave me cooped up in a bed.

What's your Name?

8ᵗʰ September Monday 2008.

There's a name on every face
And a face to every name,
It's how you recognize that
Everybody's not the same,
It determines who you are
From the day that you are born,
And it stays with you forever
Even though your body's worn,
If you try to live without it
There's no future or no fame,
No-one would even speak to you
'Cause no-one would know your name.

"Fixed Abode".

Once I lived and now I don't
Done my own thing now I won't,
Have to stay here in my grave
No matter what I cannot leave,
Got no TV, got no phone,
I just lie here all alone,
Twenty four long hours a day
Ne'er a word I cannot say,
So think of me and don't ask who
'Cause someday you will lie here too.

A Prayer.

9th September Tuesday 2008.

Lord, cleanse my heart and cleanse my soul
and cleanse my tongue and all,
Keep the sins of day at bay
So I won't sin a tall.

Do not allow the stains that stick
to every part of me,
But use your elbow grace oh Lord
so all from me will flee.

Wash out my mouth with your rough sea
to choose the words that flow from me,
Do not allow my heart to stray
and keep the evil thoughts at bay.

Above all else it's fair to say
that I will do my best today,
So on my tongue and in my soul
along with you I'll always stroll.

Of this I ask I do not beg
because you say I'll receive
Give me that little mustard seed
And help me to believe.

Unexplored Territory.

10th Sept. Wednesday 2008.

Some people travel all round the world
Exploring far off regions,
Like ancient conquerors they plod
Adding to their legions,
And yet they rarely give a thought
when covering all the map,
The territory mostly unexplored
lies directly beneath their cap.

This is a proven fact today of every body born,
The percentage it is very high
the truth to you I'll warn,
For most of us we only use a very small amount,
The rest it lies in idleness and never gives account.

But don't go blaming all the stuff
that's fixed between your ears,
The key is in ignition but "you" have to interfere,
It only starts to operate when you decide it will,
Otherwise it's satisfied to just remain there still.

Every thing today is visualised no thinking for yourself,
Just take a seat, all wrapped up neat
And sit there on the shelf,
And whilst you might deny this
maybe you don't fit the bill,
For 95 percent of us our brain's in constant chill.

One For Sorrow.

11ᵗʰ September Thursday 2008.

One for sorrow two for joy
was lumbered on the Magpie,
Three for a girl four for a boy
Left this wee bird a dragonfly,
Five for silver six for gold
A sight you'll rarely see,
Seven means the secret's safe
You could nearly guarantee.

Now if you are superstitious
and <u>Two</u> Magpies make your day,
Then you also must remember
<u>One</u> could turn your head astray,
So be careful if your life goes round
your sorrows and your joys,
Cause <u>Four</u> could strip you of a girl
and <u>Three</u> a little boy.

Now when it comes to silver,
and when it comes to gold,
Then you nearly can be certain
that no secrets will unfold,
For seeing Magpies <u>Five</u> or <u>Six</u> or <u>Seven</u> is very rare,
Unless they're fighting on your street
In the early morning air.

For one is just a loner, and two they're maybe lovers
Three or four are sisters, or maybe even brothers,
Five or six are siblings, with little cousin seven,
and none of them could give a damn
If you're in hell or heaven.

Teamwork 1963.

I watched the pair of them, one old, one young,
Their powerful legs and froth biting tongues,
No doubt without at least some pain,
Straining on the plough, tightening the chains.

The heat of the day and sweat covered hides,
With clegs sucking life blood from each horse's side,
My father's cap sliding sideways on his head,
With cigarette lit, held firmly, not a word said.

Up and down slowly, but progress quickly made,
The plough turns the earth as day starts to fade,
A rest in the furrow for the old boy, stops youth too,
A chance for dad to straighten, and light another Blue.

Off again and the young horse leads the way,
The three of them together in harmony all day,
Hands on the plough and reins held tight,
For a young lad like me, a wonderful sight.

"Come up are that," as if the horse understood,
And yet in response to father he always would,
Each one trustworthy with that command,
Happy to be driven and happy to be manned.

And so at the end of the day they stood,
All three were tired but the work was good,
Even I could see this sense of pride
as the horses yawned by my father's side.

Puzzled.

13ᵗʰ September Saturday 2008.

"What is that thing up on the wall?" my daughter said to me,
"It's a football" said the little boy,
  looking up with glee.
"Its not indeed" the big one said,
"Can't you see that it's the moon",
"You're all wrong" said the oldest girl
"Sure it's a saucer without a spoon".

Well I listened to all their comments
from the youngest one and all,
As to what this stupid object was, hanging from the wall.

"It must be the top of a chimney pot that has fallen on its side",
"It's far too big you silly girl, it's more like a revolving slide",
"It's nothing of the sort now", said the little boy again,
"Sure it must be just an object for them to catch the rain".

Well I listened to all their comments
from the youngest one and all,
As to what this stupid object was, hanging on the wall.

Well then my daughter said to me "ach daddy I know now",
"The man next door has put it there, but I just don't know how,
My wee friend told me in school that she has got one too"
And the little boy said "without it, she couldn't watch TV".

So I listened to all their comments from the youngest one and all
As to what this stupid object was hanging on the wall,
And when they all, the three of them,
Said "Oh daddy, oh we wish…"
I quickly snapped at them and said,
"No Satellite Dish".

The Dentists Chair.

14ᵗʰ September Sunday 2008.

Jimmy had an awful fear the dentists chair to sit in,
And the thoughts of someone telling him
to open up and spit in,
And laying flat upon his back his tonsils gaping out,
Was not exactly what he thought this life was all about.

But pain if it is bad enough, will overcome your fear,
Eventually you will make the move
the dentists to go near,
And when you do just be prepared
to place yourself in trust
For medical utensils such as needles are a must.

But Jimmy hadn't been for checks
for such a long, long time,
His teeth were simply rotten
he had never spent a dime,
And the news for him was very bad
the stumps would all need pulled,
This was devastating and an awful stomach full.

But that's the way it happened,
it soon would come to pass,
Jimmy took his turn, the dentists chair to plop his ass,
And when the final blow was dealt
He was in shocking pain,
He shook his head quite firmly
Saying,
"Never, Never Again!"

Contentment.

15th September Monday 2008.

There's a feeling of contentment
flowing through my veins today,
It is something strange inside me that I would not give away,
But if you should ask the question to describe the best I can,
Just what it is that started it, or how it all began.

I would have to say contentment
doesn't come from having much,
It is not the kind of feeling that's inspired by such and such,
And it does not make its way to you
by keeping scores and tabs,
It is motivated sorely by the gift of Love to grab.

It is not the kind of feeling you can buy with silver coins,
It is not a heartfelt passion you can welcome all to join,
And it's not the kind of sentiment you can simply give away,
For when it dwells inside you, it will do it's best to stay.

For contentment is spontaneous, a reaction you could say,
To a person or a place that you could stumble on today,
And you will know for certain when confronted with a task,
If you suffer from contentment by the questions you are ask.

It is measured by the way that you react within yourself,
As to whether you release the giant
or display the tender elf,
But if you can keep your temper
and repress to take command,
Then you will find contentment
will be surely close at hand.

Lesson Inhaled.

16th September Tuesday 2008.

We used to buy our cigarettes in ones and twos and threes,
In Jinny Diamond's little shop, you'd never get one free,
She always charged us thrupence each
and warned us all "Tut – Tut,
Now you get of here my boy, and keep your big mouth shut".

But this was not unusual, we could buy them anywhere,
The shops in town would split a pack without a single care,
But rules and regulations never meant a thing to us,
for we were glad to get them, with nothing to discuss.

Now, one day I got lucky and I bought myself a pack,
I had gathered up a shilling, this would save me running back,
So I put them in my pocket, and I headed up to school,
But I needed to be careful for 'No Cigs' it was the rule,

So I slipped behind the toilets, approaching dinner time,
I took a mate to puff with me like partners in crime,
When suddenly the teacher, Mc Namara was his name,
Approached us out of nowhere, and asked who was to blame.

Of course me being the leader, had to own up there and then,
He asked to see the packet, which had started out with ten,
There was no use refusing, for red handed we were caught,
He asked how much they cost me,
and where they had been bought.

But I was saying nothing, my heart began to pump
He clinched his fist with anger round the packet with a grump,
"Oh I am desperate sorry" was his only sick retort,
As he trampled my tobacco all over the tennis court.

The Visiting.

17th September Wednesday 2008.

Have you's no home to go to, I said to my three girls,
For you's seem to spend more time with us
since married life unfurled,
We do not mind you calling and it's nice to see you all,
But it's also nice to see you leave
and take your off springs, small.

It doesn't seem so long ago since you were kids yourselves,
And it only seems like yesterday
when here you used to dwell,
But one by one you took the oath to go it on your own,
Though strange enough it seems to us
You spend more time at home.

But it's always great to see you and it's great to see you go
'Cause the peace you soon get used to
when you're saying cheerio,
Now its not that we object to you're your wee visits we receive
It's just that very often "Dears" you don't know when to leave.

So I hope you're not offended by this simple little verse
Describing how we feel for now, when all of you disperse,
'Cause as I said before it's great when all of you appear
But it's always so relaxing just to see you from the rear.

Well here's hoping when you read this,
you will not bear a grudge,
But I'd be hoping when you visit
That you won't be hard to budge,
So the future can be sorted if we use our common sense,
Do not overstay your welcome when you're in our residence.

Secret Love.

18th September Thursday 2008.

Love is just the reason why I'm living,
Love is just the secret for my giving,
So the reason why I'm living
And the secret for my giving,
Is that Love for me is constantly forgiven.

Love is just the reason why I labour,
Love is my excuse to greet my neighbour,
So the reason why I labour
My excuse to love my neighbour,
Means I never get involved to lift the sabre.

Love is just the reason for my singing
Love was such a part of my upbringing,
So the reason why I sing
And the qualities I bring,
See the optimistic side of everything.

Now the Love I know is practical for me,
It's in recognising people that you see,
It's in Living, it's in Giving
It's in Labour, Neighbour too,
It's in Singing and in Bringing
"All To You".

Nonsense.

19th September Friday 2008.

One bright night in the middle of the day,
a fire broke out on the ocean,
A blind man saw it and a deaf man heard it,
And a lame man ran for the fire brigade,
The fire brigade came
pulled by two dead horses,
Run over two dead cats
and nearly half killed them,
This story was told by three dumb men
sitting at the corner of a round table,
Eating plain bread with currants in it.

Cycle Of Life.

A mans life is very short no matter what his years,
Some day he has to leave this earth
and cast aside his fears,
For what is here is definite, a light before your eyes,
The moon the stars the rising sun
they shine out from the skies,
For man is born with nothing
but the skin upon his bones,
The beginning and the end he is very much alone,
For what lies beyond is uncertain
and faith he needs to have,
For time it flies, it's just a blink
from the cradle to the grave.

Time Doesn't Wait.

20th September Saturday 2008.

When you stop to think of the speed of time,
It just disappears like an old clocks chime,
It fades away like a summer tan
Old folks say "Time waits on no man".

When you push the world in front of you,
And labour and toil till your face is blue,
It's true again what old folks say
"You just wishing and wasting
   your time away".

So stop and think every now and then,
Take a step back every now and again,
And remember once more what old folks say,
"Try to live a little along the way"

Before you know it will be over and done,
So take the time for a little fun,
And ponder back to days gone by,
When old folks even had the time to die.

So I leave you with a message true,
Just to listen what old folks say,
Experience has the upper hand
because they have had their day.

In the Final.

21ˢᵗ September Sunday 2008.

The decimal levels went through the roof on September 21ˢᵗ
The whole place just erupted when vocal cords all burst,
The feelings of euphoria were felt across the North,
Sam Maguire was on a journey
as the fans all cried "come forth".

But this would not be easy as both teams had much to gain,
On one side you had the Kingdom who much desired to reign,
But twice before Sam made this trip to visit Omagh town,
And once again the feelings were,
that he'd be homeward bound.

Now Mc Connell stood between the posts
and served his County well
Mc Mahans marked the two twin towers
And eventually would excel,
With Gormley close to Cooper closing down his two good feet,
Davy Harte against Paul Galvin a battle to compete.

Philip Jordan won the contest against strong O' Sullivan,
Mc Menamim was majestic and wiped out Brosnan,
Colin Holmes he was the weaker link
And Hughes he took his place,
Mc Ginley scored three powerful points
Tyrone were in the race.

Now when it comes to football you just have to give him praise
Brian Dooher was magnificent and left Kerry in a daze,
Well Mc Guigan and Mc Cullagh, Penrose and Mellon too
They played their parts to welcome home
This man well you know who.

We can't forget the star man, he must be made of steel
Sean Cavanagh romped headquarters, his true talents to reveal,
And just before we finish, let's remember Mickey Harte
His strategy for winning, it was simply "Very Smart"

Unrepeatable.

22nd September Monday 2008.

There is one thing on my mind today
I will have to make it clear,
Regarding all the poems that I write
throughout the year,
Because I don't look back on them
I am never really sure,
As too whether I repeat myself
I only can endure.

But there is something that I do know
from writing every day,
That it would be impossible
to repeat them anyway,
For when a line comes to your head
you need to write it down,
For forty seconds later
It has vanished from your mind.

I wrote a lovely poem once
on my computer screen,
And then one touch in Error
I wiped the whole thing clean,
Now it was gone for ever
I really could have cried,
I could not record it word for word
No matter how I tried.

Human Kindness.

When it comes to human kindness
we could all of us reveal,
The lengths that people go to
to promote the will to heal,
And nothing is a bother
for those who choose the path,
They do it with conviction
and enthusiastic craft.

Now all of us have met them
You're probably one yourself,
It's part of your ingredients
the make up of your wealth,
And if you are, be grateful
for its something you can't buy,
It's just something you've been born with
handed down in full supply.

And what a difference it all makes
to meet someone today,
Who's keen to make things happen
in a special kind of way,
Now when everything around you
seems to plunge and take a dive,
Just let the wagon pass you by
for the world will still survive.

Colum.

24th September Wednesday 2008.

He's a typical example of what a Priest should be,
There's no such thing as boredom no-one could disagree,
He's a servant of his people and yet he's not a slave,
Transparent in his actions he is always very brave.

He impresses all the young ones his presence it is sound,
And includes the Gospel message he never waters down,
And they can all approach him in human frame to frame,
He tries to get to know them all,
and call them by their name.

Well he is very active with the parish at the front,
He tries to make decisions and keep up with the hunt,
He meets with the committees and all is ironed out,
Then follows up with action no need to yell or shout.

Now when it comes to old folks he's always on the ball,
He makes a point to visit them and bring a prayerful call,
And anyone who's housebound he listens to their pleas,
And helps to brighten up their day, a spiritual guarantee.

If you should need to share a thought in quiet confidence,
If you desire to listen then just give this man a chance,
For you will find a willingness to relate to all your ways,
And you'll feel all the better for his dropping in today.

Now when it comes to Parish life he's happy to be here,
He's full of his vocation and creates an atmosphere,
The community all around us,
they respond with true support,
To help them on a mission on a journey to escort.

Delivery Suite.

25th September Thursday 2008.

Paddy's wife was pregnant and her time was drawing near,
He dropped her at maternity saying "it's time I wasn't here"
For he was surely adamant that the birth he would not see
Yes, Paddy was convinced it was not the place to be.

And despite the voices raised they were not of his concern,
To watch his wife in agony it would only make him squirm,
So he cautioned to the midwife for a minute on her own,
Not to burden him with pressure, just to call him on the phone.

But Paddy got impatient as the time it lingered on,
So deciding he would make a move, he phoned the Mid head on,
But on his mobile phone he hit a three and not a four,
He rang the cricket club instead, asked her "what's the score?"

Now the lady on the other end her head was on the blink,
She said "it's only started" but she never stopped to think,
There's three out now already, and a fourth one's on the way,
It looks as if it's going to be, a very busy day.

Well suddenly the sweat began to run down Paddy's face,
He dropped his mobile phone, and his tail began to chase,
And in his terrible trauma he was overcome with guilt,
How he could be so reckless, his poor wife he could jilt.

So Paddy in a panic he raced to the delivery suite,
His wife was sitting in the bed all tucked up nice and neat,
And holding out her arms to him she said here's your wee son,
And before you start to worry, "I only had the one".

Problems On Board.

26ᵗʰ September Friday 2008.

When you expand to meet demand
you need to take on board,
As well as all the good times
all the problems you will hoard.
For bigger isn't always, a better place to be,
There's always competition
and there's nothing trouble free.

When you expand to meet demand
more bodies make the payroll,
You may be getting much more done
but you've less and less control,
Now the outputs may be higher
and more customers get their stuff,
But when looking for the payment
they can start to huff and puff.

So if you have upped the aunty
to increase your business plan,
If you have spent more money
to supply to meet demand,
Then lookout for what the profits say
when the overheads hit the roof,
You may not be much better off
but the books will tell the truth.

Abortion.

27th September Saturday 2008.

God I hate that word Abortion
It's a name that I deplore,
It makes the hair stand on my neck
like nothing has before,
In all the years that's passed now
since David Steele's bad bill,
We've all been made to swallow
that rotten bitter pill.

For millions they have died now
since that first bill was passed,
To satisfy the lustful ways
of all which ever class,
It's forty years ago now
when the government choose to slay,
So many innocent children
never seen the light of day.

How anyone on both sides
could inflict such terrible pain,
On these totally, little perfect
and defenceless human beings.

Just Not To Be.

28th September Sunday 2008.

I can only imagine what life would be like
If I had walked in another direction,
Going back to the days when I was only sixteen
To a life of love and affection,
For my papers were signed to a navel career
And the ships of a merchant collection,
But divine intervention you could say played a part
When I failed to make the selection.

But back in the days of my youth you could say
When careers were the height of infection,
You were sucked automatically into the pipe
Without a great deal of inspection,
And most of us fell into the trap of success
The focus was not on reflection,
So in the spur of the hour a teenage desire
There wasn't the time for correction.

So the future for me it was signed up and sealed
There wasn't a cause for objection,
But I never thought for the moment I sought
That I would suffer rejection,
But I'll never know I can only imagine
Not likely to my satisfaction,
Why I was refused a place in the sun
Why I didn't live up to perfection.

Silver Lining.

29th September Monday 2008.

I believe inside each cloud a silver lining lies,
And the more you try to reach it
Then the more it satisfies,
It's there in opportunity
when the preparation's done,
So try hard not to miss it
for it never may return.

I believe inside each cloud a silver lining lies,
It's just waiting for the moment
To release its self and fly,
So be careful with your longings
And choose well your desires,
Now be watchful when your eyes blink
It could set your heart on fire.

I believe inside each cloud a silver lining lies,
I also have this feeling that
It's there in full supply,
So please, do not be too disheartened
When you think you're feeling down,
There is always a silver lining
When your life is upside down.

Tick Tock.

30th September Tuesday 2008.

Another day is nearly gone
Daylight begins to go,
It doesn't seem like sixteen hours,
From I heard the rooster crow.

Another week is almost gone
"It's Friday" says I,
It seems no time since Monday morn
As the days just roll on by.

Another year is almost gone
The calendar says it all,
We stroke each day off with a tick
And the tock is on the wall.

Another decade passes by
As we struggle and we strive,
I seem to know more people dead
Than I ever knew alive.

A score of years is nothing now
When you reach a certain age,
But you soon begin to realise
The need to disengage.

October

Titles Of Poems   *Month of October*

There'll Be More	1st October	Wednesday	2008
The Halo	2nd October	Thursday	2008
Early Rising	3rd October	Friday	2008
The Weekend	4th October	Saturday	2008
Kindness	5th October	Sunday	2008
What Is???	6th October	Monday	2008
The Mouse	7th October	Tuesday	2008
Credit Crunch	8th October	Wednesday	2008
Wishing	9th October	Thursday	2008
I'm Always Right	10th October	Friday	2008
In God's Hands	11th October	Saturday	2008
The Cats Lick	12th October	Sunday	2008
"The Lotto"	13th October	Monday	2008
Horse Power	14th October	Tuesday	2008
Times Ticken On	15th October	Wednesday	2008
A Long Night	16th October	Thursday	2008
Poetic Inspiration	17th October	Friday	2008
"Do Today"	18th October	Saturday	2008
Sunday Worship	19th October	Sunday	2008
Topics	20th October	Monday	2008
Famous Animals	21st October	Tuesday	2008
Young As Feel	22nd October	Wednesday	2008
Full Irish	23rd October	Thursday	2008
Breed Like Rabbits	24th October	Friday	2008

Made To Be Sold	25th October	Saturday	2008
Root Of All Evil	26th October	Sunday	2008
Fill Your Tank	27th October	Monday	2008
Wee Jimmy	28th October	Tuesday	2008
The Badger	29th October	Wednesday	2008
Wagging Tongues	30th October	Thursday	2008
Scratch My Back	31st October	Friday	2008

There'll Be More.

1ˢᵗ October Wednesday 2008.

I have only three months left to go
for a poem every day,
At this point I'm determined
to create a passageway,
That will take me on a journey
that I know will shake my skills,
For to latch on new material
if this dream I should fulfil.

And even though I've struggled
through this year now every day,
There has always been a poem or a verse, along the way,
But I never realised when I started out back then,
Of the shear amount of days involved, in tuning up my pen.

But here I am October, I am truly glad to see,
And although I have been challenged
I've enjoyed this writing spree,
And the trails and tribulations, I have faced along the way,
Were unforeseen for certain, way back - last New Year's day.

As I start off in this tenth month, to write another verse,
I am trying to put on paper
something new and nothing worse,
But what that is I do not know
we'll have to wait and see,
Just wait in expectation
There'll be more I guarantee.

The Halo.

2nd October Thursday 2008.

A Halo is a circle that's suspended in the air,
And it's not the kind of thing
that you would see just anywhere,
But they say that you would see it
up above a saintly head,
Something that is very scarce
and is very rarely bred.

But it's been known to happen
and I'm sure we all know one,
A person who is very good
and deserves their praises won,
And it's a worthy statement
and a compliment at that,
To procure a fitting comment
if you're fit to wear that hat.

But it's always worth remembering
about a Halo above your head,
It sits about twelve inches up beyond
where you are fed,
And if you are unlucky
and your fortunes you misuse,
It only has to drop a bit
and it becomes a noose.

Early Rising.

3rd October Friday 2008.

When you get the name of early rising
You can lie all day,
This was an old expression
My father used to say,
And to put it into context
It described a lazy man,
Someone who could bluff his way
And always chance his arm.

For he created this impression
That he was always on the ball,
He'd be seen in certain places
Where he would not be at all,
And yet he would be seen to be
A leader in the pack,
But he was good at delegating
Whilst he himself, he was laidback.

Maybe you're the kind of person
Who is always to the front,
Yet when all the pressure tally's
You are never in the hunt,
Everybody thinks you're busy
By the way you bluff your way,
When you get the name of early rising
You can lie all day.

The Weekend.

4th October Saturday 2008.

Saturdays are always days that I look forward to,
Sometimes it almost seems as if
those days are very few,
But when everyday's a pressure
with a schedule to the fore,
There's always this release valve
waiting there in store.

For Mondays up to Fridays
tramp the paths of deadlines met,
Those forty hours producing stuff, in and out of debt,
And whilst there's certain satisfaction
going along this beaten track,
That Friday evening feeling means that Saturday is back.

Now I would have to say for sure that I can feel the calm,
When four o'clock on Friday comes
this urge to just disarm,
And put aside the urgent need to fill the days up full,
Well Saturday is a blessing, this day's so valuable.

So I will have to say to you that Saturday is my day,
And even there's some loose ends
that never go away,
I always feel a winding down that's difficult to explain,
But it comes round now once a week
And helps to keep me sane.

Kindness.

There's always this thing about kindness
when you keep trying to give it away,
For no matter how much you decide to offload
the returns they will always outweigh.

For kindness it may be a virtue,
and be loving, considerate and true,
But the more you keep giving to others
then the more it returns onto you.

Now you may be willing to loose it,
It's not worth the effort you see,
In fact it would be more convenient,
if it disappeared, A.S.A.P.

Sometimes you don't want to be bothered,
It's hard to get through a long day,
Without having to deal with this kindness,
and the effort of giving it away.

It's unfortunate if you have this problem,
where kindness keeps coming to you,
But if giving is just in your nature
Then the interest will always pursue.

What Is ???

6th October Monday 2008.

What is life if it's not about living?
What is living if it's not about giving?
What is giving if it's not about receiving?
What is receiving if it's not about accepting?
What is accepting if it's not about being thankful?
What is being thankful if it doesn't respond?
Why respond if you're not feeling thankful?
Why be thankful if you do not mean it?

If you do not mean it then do not say it.
If you can not say it then do not try.
If you do not try it you'll never know.
If you do not know it then live in the dark.
If you live in the dark you'll not see the light.
If you don't see the light you'll miss the day.
If you miss the day you'll miss the night.
If you miss the night you'll miss the morn.
If you miss the morn you'll miss the dawn.

If there's some of this in your daily life,
and you find that it's all a chore,
Then do not be too disheartened
or it will haunt you all the more,
Just make a little effort and that will sort it out,
By believing in your struggles
you can wipe out all your doubt.

The Mouse.

7th October Tuesday 2008.

I remember once our cat caught a mouse
and the two of them played outside our house,
Well the mouse stood up on its two back legs
and it wasn't the kind of stance that begs.
Well one to one he faced that cat
with legs in the air like an acrobat,
I imagined him with boxing gloves
just ready to smack that cat above.
But every now and then that mouse
would seem to take cold feet,
And thinking he would not be missed
he chooses his right to creep,
But a slowly outstretched paw would stop
that poor little mouse did a belly flop,
And just when you'd think his life was gone
he'd bounce up again and carry on,
Well this went on for at least an hour
to resolve the thing was beyond my power,
Till finally the game it came to an end
no paw of friendship would extend,
A relationship could never grow
for the mouse he was no Romeo,
So in my haste to look away
my eyes they left the trail,
When I returned all I could see
was a disappearing tail.

Credit Crunch.

8th October Wednesday 2008.

This poem that I'm writing now
reflects the present time,
With financial institutions rapidly in decline,
For they've invested all our money
In a world that's revolving round,
With too many expectations
for an increase in the pound.

Well they've invested it in companies
In silver, oil and gold,
With many too top heavy
Executives on the roll,
And bit by bit they've ate away
their profits all wrapped up,
By all the big fat cats employed
They're drinking from the cup.

But times they are a changing
and the crunch is felt by all,
With money disappearing
and with stock shares on the fall,
And this affects each one of us
with savings on the line,
But like it all or lump it,
everything is in decline.

Wishing.

9th October Thursday 2008.

Sometimes he'd ask me to take him for a walk
or take him fishing,
Looking back now all I'm left with
are hours and hours of wishing,
Wishing I had taken the time to spend an hour with him,
The simple little things just filled his life up to the brim.

But I was awful busy then and I was always in demand,
And because of all my talents
then good wages I'd command,
There was never once a thought
came to my mind to slow it down,
But somewhere in the middle I forgot
this little clown.

Sometimes when I'd come in at night
my lad would be in bed,
And then with early mornings
I would miss his ginger head,
A full week it could pass so fast
and my contact would fall short,
The walks, the fishing, had to wait for I was overwrought.

But now I wish with deep regret
that I could wind it back,
For I would turn it upside down
a different nut I'd crack,
It's over now and can't be done my lad he passed away,
A sudden illness ended all one busy summers day.

I'm Always Right.

10th October Friday 2008.

It's easy to be critical and to judge another's word,
It is a matter of opinion but his is just absurd,
Spoken out of knowledge he wouldn't have a clue,
Put in a position he would not know what to do.

You know I have this feeling that he is always wrong,
If you want my impression don't bring him along,
Some of us we know the way, we've been there before,
Let him speak his mind, but simply just ignore.

For we can make decisions you and me and us,
But when it comes to Tom and Joe nobody will trust,
So let them have their little say spoil them if you will,
But when the chatter's over cook them on the grille.

All of us we do this every single day,
We even judge our neighbour in everything they say,
But more so when at meetings, if we happen to be there,
We can always flog the donkey, despite another's prayer,

Well in this piece of writing the time to judge is gone,
I want to wipe it out for good
and tackle it head on,
And share with you this little line
I hope the words will stay,
For a clock that hasn't went for years
"Is still right twice a day"!

In God's Hands.

11ᵗʰ October Saturday 2008.

On this October Saturday the sun has chased the rain,
And when the weather changes everybody gains,
Well all of us are blessed in ways that God is on patrol,
Just think of all chaos if men were in control.

It doesn't bear to think about if man could call the shots,
When it comes to share the elements
they would all be casting lots,
They would float them on the markets
Stocks and shares and bonds,
And all of them would charge us
for to wave their magic wands.

Now some of us would get the rain
and some would get the sun,
And you could have this argument
it's already being done,
But stop to think if men could sway
and change the weather every day,
We would be in some position then
for only some could pay.

For some would bask in selfishness
the sun would fill their day,
And some would be in lifeboats
and be simply washed away,
That is why the weather will always be with God
He would never dream of leaving it
To any human squad.

The Cat's Lick.

My Daddy rarely had a bath throughout his adult days,
You could say a phobia was built into his ways,
Was he scared of water, or the fear of being clean?
Well let me tell you neither, or rather in between.

Now he would always steep his feet
when his labouring day was done,
He put some table salt into the water just for fun,
Well that's what he would say to us,
but now I know he lied,
He used it for a reason, it was always justified.

His feet were never sweaty
when he took them from his boots,
He said the pores were open the salt he would salute,
And he always had this passion
if his feet were sweet and clean,
That the rest of all your body
would be somewhere in between.

When Daddy he was growing up,
there was no such thing,
A bath it was a luxury reserved for queen and king,
Of course he never knew that, so wiser he was not,
A cat's lick in a basin was the only wash he got.

So when my Dad grew older he continued in his ways,
I always can remember one of his oul sayings,
When he was asked the question to put him on the spot,
He said he bathed yearly, whether he needed it or not.

"The Lotto".

13ᵗʰ October Monday 2008.

They say that all the friends you have
could double up or more,
If you should win the lotto
or fortune knock your door,
For some of them were backward
and some of them were shy,
The ones you haven't seen for years
and never told you why.
But suddenly they all appear
and want to wish you well,
Maybe scrape a pound or two
and hang round for a spell.
Now I don't know for certain
if there's truth in what I say,
If friends come from the woodwork
to wish you well today,
For I have never won the lotto
and I have never won the pools,
So if I have long lost cousins
then we never met at school,
But there's one thing I can tell you
if I should win ten million pounds,
For all the extra friends I'd have
I'll be glad to share it around.

Horse Power.

14ᵗʰ October Tuesday 2008.

There's an awful lot of talk shows, about the latest cars,
The makes, the shapes, the colours,
 to suit the biggest stars,
And they focus on the rpm and the nought to sixty speed,
The rules and regulations they never seem to heed.

What lies beneath the bonnet they always let you know,
Bunged up with many horses, to make this mad thing go,
It always is a selling point the faster it will boot,
Top speed the ton and over, new drivers to recruit.

Now if you go to car shows there's no end to the spend,
They go to any lengths they need to try and recommend,
That this is just the car for you all glass and plastic too,
Forget about the old ones and buy yourself anew.

Now I won't be a spoilsport for I like a decent car,
But when it comes to talk shows, I think they go too far,
For it simply isn't possible to drive the way they say,
The law would gather you all up
and throw the keys away.

It just promotes a danger that young ones can't resist,
To have the latest model and become a motorist,
But to over ride the paddle, power steering in your hand,
Is asking for disaster many do not understand.

It was listening to the radio, one day I heard transmit,
That horsepower was much safer
When Horses Only Had it!

Time's Ticken On.

15ᵗʰ October Wednesday 2008.

The length of a day is amazingly short
it's a topic on every ones tongue,
A concern that's expressed from those who are old
to those who are exceedingly young.

So each generation has something to say
there's no use in trying to ignore,
It seems to be talked about, more often today
than I can remember before.

"The time it is flying" is a favourite one,
as common a verse you would hear,
"The day's only a blink" is how people think
and it constantly rings in your ear.

"Time's ticken on" you would hear now and then
from those who are busy in life,
"Time it is money" is the cry you would hear
from the sufferers of strain, stress and strife.

Now since all this began "Time waits on no man"
the faster the time seems to go,
There is never a day that passes my way
someone says that the days going slow,
Yet the clock is the same I will have to exclaim
when our parents were rearing us all,
but the panic we pledge to live on the edge
means time, it is always on call.

A Long Night.

16th October Thursday 2008.

One lonely night after another
I have lay staring into the dark,
With the shadows there just to remind me
and the sound of a lonesome dog bark.

I looked for a while at the window
the moon trying to shine through the blind,
The thoughts of the world running past me
with nothing but sleep on my mind.

And yet I was tortured and restless
as tired as a fox on the run,
Just trying to escape the commotion
and wishing the night would be done.

A spider appears from the ceiling
in silence it climbs down its web,
I decide should I get up and kill it
but I can't, so I stay here in bed.

First sheep, I will count to a hundred
my conscience I'll strip to the bone,
The night that is passing so slowly
is as precious as any I've known.

Poetic Inspiration.

17th October Friday 2008.

If I can write poems then anyone can
'Cause I'm just an ordinary kind of a man,
I have no idea when all this began
I thought when it started
'twas a flash in the pan.

But if you consider the verses I write
It's not rocket science this stuff I recite,
It's simply ideas I have day and night
and hopefully they
will wet your appetite.

Words are good therapy once they are written
the more you record the more you are smitten,
You get to the stage you love to be sitting,
Just reporting on things
From kittens to knitting.

So if you ever thought of becoming a poet,
You could be one now and simply not know it,
Just grab a Bic pen a test to your wit,
Allow your brain flow
and let it transmit.

"Do Today".

18th October Saturday 2008.

You can never tell
when your fortunes could change
and leave you like a tramp in the street,
You can never tell
in the course of your journey
Who you might happen to meet.

You never can say when your life takes a turn
what road you could end up upon,
You never can say in a junction of life
when all of your treasures are gone.

So don't be afraid to make a wee change
if you think there are changes to make,
Don't be afraid to abandon old ways
if you think there are habits to break.

And don't be afraid to confine to the dust
the anchors that pull your life down,
All of the ones that give you such pain
and constantly cause you to frown.

For no one can do what you do for yourself
it's a task you can't delegate,
So take up the mantle and do it today
for tomorrow it might be too late.

Sunday Worship.

That Sunday feeling it comes over me
the urge to go to church,
It's there I've been for years now
on the third seat back I perch,
I rarely ever missed a time
on the seventh day of the week,
When I was not involved someway
the grace of God to seek.

Now we were started early
and on Sundays we would walk,
Down the Scarva Road
up on the footpath we would talk,
Well this became a habit
and began when we were young,
But it always was compulsory
go to Mass and hold your tongue.

And so your parents train you
despite yourself or not,
You form your life around them
and some things are not forgot,
In ways it is a good thing
there's a challenge in your time,
It always helps remind you
Life is not a pantomime.

Topics.

Sometimes it's hard to capture things
and you'll say sure it's not worthwhile,
They can seem so unimportant
you won't bother to compile.

But later on you stop to think
and you surely wish you had
There's always value in the past
no matter good or bad.

For a lot of things go through your head
and your torn what to write
You can't decide on politics
or world wars that are rife.

Now there's hunger and starvation
you could record them all the time,
There's pay offs and redundancies
and constant scenes of crime.

So I think I'll stick to humour
Well, at least for a day or so,
And hopefully won't annoy myself
In a world that's full of woe.

Famous Animals.

21ˢᵗ October Tuesday 2008.

Delaney had a donkey
and McGinty had a goat,
The donkey it went missing
'cause the goat it ate the rope.

Delaney had a donkey
and McGinty had a goat,
McDonald had a farmyard,
it looked like Noah's Boat.

Delaney had a donkey
and McGinty had a goat,
It was about the two of them
that great songwriters wrote.

Delaney had a donkey
and McGinty had a goat,
one was good at kicking
to pen the famous quote.

But Delaney won no Derbys
and McGinty got black tea,
It would seem they both were useless
That's just the way things be's.

Young As You Feel.

22nd October Wednesday 2008.

You are only as young as you feel
this response I was given from Jim,
Implying that looks are misleading
well, that was the answer from him.

You are only as young as you feel
this response I was given from Bob,
Don't judge this old book by its cover,
right now I just feel like a slob.

You are only as young as you feel
this response I was given from Bill,
Be careful when making your comments
of compliments I've had quite a fill.

You are only as young as you feel
this response I was given from John,
What's taking its toll on the inside
And the parts that are going and gone.

But George, when I asked for an answer,
Was more cautious and slow to reveal,
But pressurised into responding, said,
You're as young as the woman you feel!

Full Irish.

23rd October Thursday 2008

A full Irish breakfast is the offer on the plate
between the hours of seven and eleven, don't be late,
There's lots of fruit and orange juice
and there's cornflakes by the box,
To loosen up your taste buds
there's porridge for goldilocks.

Now when you've eaten up your fill
and have little room for more,
"Have you ordered?" comes the question
from the waitress on the floor,
We have sausage, egg and bacon
and delicious mushrooms too
Black pudding and tomatoes,
and a pot of Irish brew.

Now the toast is of the freshest
the bread is white and brown,
If you want another helping,
we will gladly bring it down.
There's marmalade and butter so just you help yourself
and plenty more stock piled up on the pantry shelf.

Well, this will always happen
when I'm on that weekend break,
I eat enough for two of us till I have bellyache,
Yet this only seems to happen when I go away and roam
for I never eat a breakfast when I am back at home.

Breed Like Rabbits.

24th October Friday 2008.

Now the teacher asked young Michael
when he was doing his sums,
To give a simple answer to
the question one plus one,
This is not a tricky problem now
the young lad jumped up quick,
Says Michael, "Miss it's twenty two
I'm good at arithmetic!"

So the teacher asked young Michael
to explain to all the class,
How he cumbered up his answer
and he'd better do it fast,
He said, "my father bought a rabbit
and my mother bought one too,
And believe me, Miss, I counted them
for sure there's twenty two".

Well I can think of this young Michael
and put figures all together,
For we have had a cat or two
survived all kinds of weather,
and whilst we don't have rabbits
I'm inclining to agree,
Based on having the same habits
one and one I can't guarantee.

Made To Be Sold.

25ᵗʰ October Saturday 2008.

Everything you buy today
is not as good as old,
It's not made to be used they say
but it's only made to be sold,
For if you bought a cooker or an iron long ago,
They were far much more reliable
it's a proven fact you know.

Well you have to be so careful now
no matter what you buy,
For when you get it home you know
you'll break it if you try,
For every thing is flimsy,
It's so cosy and so warm,
All wrapped up neatly in a box
won't come to any harm.

But take it out and use it
and be sure to say a prayer,
For it's probably christened China
and could be the worse for wear,
For I believe for certain
stuff is not as good as old,
in fact I know for certain
it's made -- only to be sold.

Root Of All Evil.

26ᵗʰ October Sunday 2008.

Did you ever ask yourself the question,
Was money the punishment for mans sin
You know going back to the Garden of Eden
When man threw God's laws in the bin.

Did you ever ask yourself the question,
Maybe more so today than ever before
Conversations revolve round this topic
What the future has lined up in store.

For God gave us all that we needed
With the trees and the seeds and the fruit
With the beasts and the birds all around us
All these gifts we could never dispute.

And yet we are screwed up with money
It rules every breath that we take
Comparisons with dollars and sterling
The world on its axis it shakes.

Now the big institutions will crumble
All the lenders and banks they will fail
All because of this "Root of all evil"
Many won't live to tell of the tale.

Fill Your Tank.

27ᵗʰ October Monday 2008.

Make sure before you go to bed
to always fill your tank,
And if you may some day you'll say
my little poem thank,
For you never know what happens
in the middle of the night,
Any unexpected episodes
before the break of light.

Now don't be caught out napping
when a crisis should unfold,
And don't you dare insinuate
that you were never told,
For I will give you warning
this can happen anyone,
It's a very nasty moment
you discover you have none.

So don't just say you'll leave it
that tomorrow's another day,
Slip down to the nearest station,
do it now without delay,
For if you get a phone call
before the night is through,
You will rue it when the Empty sign
lights up the dash for you.

Wee Jimmy.

28ᵗʰ October Tuesday 2008.

Jimmy delivered papers on his bicycle every day,
He would take a quiet moment
at the church to stop and pray,
But the Priest up in the parochial house
was suspicious more and more,
Seeing Jimmy drop his bicycle
and run up to the door,
For he only stayed a moment
and he'd run back down the steps,
Was he stealing money from the poor box in his cap?

So the Priest he hid his presence in the church one rainy day,
And he waited for wee Jimmy
just to see if he would pray,
Well he was so amazed when the door flung open wide,
Seeing this wee skinny paper boy
run up to Jesus side,
"Jesus this is Jimmy" then he turned upon his heel,
The P.P was astounded his guilt he could not heal.

Now later on that morning
when the Priest was on his rounds,
He attended poor wee Jimmy lying on the ground,
For a car had struck his bicycle
and left him there for dead,
The Priest he knelt beside him
and he held wee Jimmy's head,
Now he claims he heard for certain
a voice so loud and clear,
"Jimmy, this is Jesus"
as it whispered in his ear.

The Badger.

29th October Wednesday 2008.

I always think that badgers often get a very raw deal,
You seem to see them lying dead
for the Magpies, just a meal,
Because they see so poorly, they are victims all the time,
Trying to cross the road for them
is dangerous, there's no signs.

No matter where you drive the roads
You're sure to see one dead,
Maybe youngsters back at home waiting to be fed,
I always feel so sorry when I see one on its side,
No trace of a damage mark showing on its hide.

But just a little knock is all it takes upon the head,
To kill this lovely animal, another badger dead.
And often they will lie there till they're all cut up in bits,
Fossilized by heavy lorries, a thousand gory hits.

A cause for no concern by all
who chance to pass their way,
Unnoticed by commuters
driving homewards every day,
And even though it may have been
your car that done the harm,
It would not keep you wakened
Or even break your sense of calm.

So slow down on your driving
for they cannot stand a clout,
And spare a thought for badgers
if you think there's some about.

Wagging Tongues.

30th October Thursday 2008.

I can always remember back
to the days when we were young,
Our parents had a crack or two
with the neighbours waggled tongues,
But before they started talking
we were told to go outside,
There was no such thing as listening,
made no difference if we cried.

But nowadays it's different,
children listen every word,
Butt into conversations
and insist that they be heard,
They will interrupt their parents
and make comments of their own,
And no-one seems to tell them
to get out until they've grown.

And so they are old fashioned
little people with big ears,
Honing in to adult voices,
worldly news and grown up fears,
And it goes to show the changes
there has been since we were young,
For this never would have happened
when our parents were wagging tongues.

Scratch My Back.

31st October Friday 2008.

There are thousands of old sayings
and we use them every day,
There are all kinds of expressions
that our mouths put on display,
But there always was a famous one
it was used by rich and poor,
To describe the goings on of those
whose lives looked so secure.

Well I heard it many, many times
since I was young at heart,
You give my back a scratch my boy
and you'll be playing smart,
And all you'll have to do for me
Is play along because,
"You scratch my back and I'll scratch yours"

Well I suppose there was an argument
for getting all things done,
And by using this arrangement
the ball was rolling, it begun.
And I'm not sure this happens now
so often as before,
For it seems to take a lifetime
to perform the simplest chores.

November

Titles of Poems　　　*Month of November*

Chinese Meals	1st November	Saturday	2008
Live Not Learn	2nd November	Sunday	2008
Wise Words	3rd November	Monday	2008
Never Too Late	4th November	Tuesday	2008
A Leg For Dinner	5th November	Wednesday	2008
Rude Awakenings	6th November	Thursday	2008
Big Family	7th November	Friday	2008
Hard Of Hearing	8th November	Saturday	2008
Time Heals	9th November	Sunday	2008
The Sermon	10th November	Monday	2008
Commercial Channel	11th November	Tuesday	2008
Don't Blame God	12th November	Wednesday	2008
Dead Watch	13th November	Thursday	2008
"POSH"	14th November	Friday	2008
"Current" Times	15th November	Saturday	2008
Reflection	16th November	Sunday	2008
The Entrepreneur	17th November	Monday	2008
Still Of Night	18th November	Tuesday	2008
Perfect Parents	19th November	Wednesday	2008
Hay Making	20th November	Thursday	2008
End Of An Era	21st November	Friday	2008
"Mum"	22nd November	Saturday	2008
The Unspeakable	23rd November	Sunday	2008

Generous To A Fault	24th November	Monday	2008
Christians	25th November	Tuesday	2008
Captured	26th November	Wednesday	2008
The Wife	27th November	Thursday	2008
Anguish	28th November	Friday	2008
The Twins	29th November	Saturday	2008
Be A Devil	30th November	Sunday	2008

Chinese Meals.

1ˢᵗ November Saturday 2008.

There are classic Chinese proverbs
which describe the way they eat,
And it simply sets out different ways
for them to scoff their meat,
For it goes back through the centuries
to the times of Cain and Abel,
They eat anything with legs
Except of course a table.

There are classic Chinese proverbs
as to how they eat a meal,
And it simply sets out different ways
the truth I will reveal,
For the diet they are used to
would drive most of us insane,
They eat anything with wings
except an aeroplane.

They eat anything that has a tongue
except of course a shoe,
And everything that has an ear
except from me and you,
But there is a Chinese proverb
which I heard the other day,
"Do not do as I do, but do as I say".

Live Not Learn.

2nd November Sunday 2008.

Sometimes I truly wonder, as my life it passes through,
If I have gained experience, in all I say and do,
For sometimes I am stupid, mistakes happen over again,
It seems to me in writing this,
"You live and never learn".

For many times I've stopped and said
why did I go down that road,
Did I not pray in bygone days
to save me from this load?
Yet here I am, like a slaughtered lamb,
in the middle of this blasted thing,
My life it just repeats itself,
recovering from the same damn sting.

And why that is I cannot say, pursuing every day,
Some things I said for definite,
I would surly throw away,
Convinced in times of struggling
this will never happen again,
Yet here I go it's happened
why can't I just refrain?
So now I know for certain
I might as well adjourn,
For I am just convinced now,
That "You live and never learn"

Wise Words.

3rd November Monday 2008.

I remember once I heard a man
his words were very wise,
He spoke about succeeding, in this life to win the prize,
He talked about the pressures
when you're aiming for the sky,
He said sometimes you need to let a few things pass you by.

If at first you don't succeed maybe you should just give in,
Take a lead, your instincts heed
you know you'll never win.
For some things are impossible, it's the all elusive dream,
You try to imitate someone
to fit into the team.

But life is not that easy, and not all will reach the top,
Along the way I have to say
that many will face the chop,
For it can sweep you off your feet,
or fill you with despair,
You need to know to take it slow
for not everything is fair.

So maybe you are trying to succeed
In some one way,
I'm not saying you are wrong,
or to give up every day,
But try to just remember
if you think it won't work out,
It may be nature telling you
to rinse it down the spout.

Never Too Late.

4th November Tuesday 2008.

I wish to God I'd started writing many years ago,
For a lot of things escaped me
I missed the boat I know,
And even though I always wrote a verse or two back then,
I never took it seriously
and for me that was a shame.

For writing is mysterious and strange when you're in touch,
It's really unbelievable how your head can hold so much,
But it's always something, someone else, is taking up to do,
And not the kind of thing you try to capture, me and you.

But I would like to change all that and challenge one and all,
Take up the gauntlet now today and have yourself a ball,
Just write about the birds the bees and everything you see,
You'll find that it won't bother you to try and copy me.

Now it never will be perfect so just try and let it grow,
If you had never written it then you would never know,
For I wish that I had started when my youth was on my side,
For it becomes a struggle when your world is bleary eyed.

Leg For Dinner.

5th November Wednesday 2008.

The farmer had a problem
every Christmas this is true,
For his wife she loved a turkey leg
but he would love one too,
To add to all his problems now
their son was just as fond,
Between the turkey leg and him
there was a favourite bond.

Well he had this great idea
to resolve his problem so,
To breed three legged turkeys
he would strive to undergo,
And then from one big turkey
they each could eat a leg,
It never would be necessary
to sit around and beg.

So Christmas came and Christmas went
big turkeys filled their yard,
The farmer and his wife and son
had bodies bruised and scarred,
The wife and son were adamant,
that daddy was to blame
For it was just impossible
to catch three legged game.

Rude Awakening.

6th November Thursday 2008.

Early one fine morning I was wakened from my sleep,
I turned my head quite slowly on the clock I had a peep,
Well it was aggravating when I tell you what went on,
A big black fly persisted on my nose to land upon.

At first I simply tried to blow to see if it would go,
But this was so annoying for your mouth is well below,
And it was far too early to give in and rise from bed,
So I lifted up my arm and tried to beat it off instead.

But the blasted fly was far too quick and every time I missed,
I hit my nose an awful clout and cursed this anarchist,
But it was all in vain for me I had to just give in,
At half past four one morning I arose my soul too sin.

Well I went and got a paper and I folded it up well,
I chased that bloody fly around the room I'll surly tell,
And not an idle moment did I spend until it fell,
My anger was contented when I said "Now rot in hell".

Big Family.

When Mary got herself a man, it was back in different days,
And trying to keep yourself warmed up
was done in different ways,
For there wasn't any heating, blasting out in every room,
To think some went to bed for heat,
I only can presume.

But it is an explanation why the family grew so big,
To have an even football team was not a deliberate rig,
And having fifteen children was a common family size,
In fact sometimes the father didn't even realise.

Well Johnny he was asked one day of the size his family grew
He turned in true amazement and he said he never knew
But the wife was always pregnant every year it was the same
Exactly what was causing it he could not ascertain.

But, she had two three times he said,
Yes, three times she had two,
And two times she had also three
of that I'll guarantee,
But when it comes to numbers
It's a difficult one you see,
And having one a whole lot of times
Was a lot of fun for me.

Hard Of Hearing.

8th November Saturday 2008.

Well now this one's most unusual
but I heard it from a friend,
And I know he is trustworthy
on his word I can depend,
For he gave me his opinion
why his family was so large,
He said his wife "Her hearing aid,
she never would recharge".

Well I was taken back by this
and of course I was confused,
So I asked him to explain to me
'cause I was not amused,
In facts I had my doubts
about his word I must admit,
But he assured me kindly
'twas the truth he would transmit.

Now he said that he would leave out
all the intimates, he would miss,
But every night he turned
to his wee wife to give a kiss,
I simply asked the question
"will we go to sleep or what?"
She always looked into my eyes
and replied to me with "WHAT"...

The Sermon.

9th November Sunday 2008.

Two preacher men they met one day
their sermons to compare,
They each had different stories
as to how they would prepare,
For each had a country parish
where the men kept cows and sheep,
The problem was on Sundays
they all would fall asleep.

Now one he had a problem
it would drive him to despair,
For he spent most of Saturday
his sermon to prepare,
But most of it was wasted
looking down at dreary eyes,
He could have shouted anything
or told a bunch of lies.

But the other was more confident
and of his congregation too,
How to keep them all awakened
he knew exactly what to do,
For most of them were farmers
he just tried a different slant,
When their eyelids they were heavy
he would simply shout
    Lord "Grant".....

Time Heals.

10th November Monday 2008.

The last five months have been a difficult time
and the truth I have to say,
That I have some amount of pain
to cope with every day,
Now the physical pain is one thing
and the healing process slow,
But it also affects you mentally,
it's the side that doesn't show.

There's a lot of external healing
to return you back to health,
Making you appreciate how much your health's your wealth,
But again you have the inward stuff,
the wounds you cannot see,
The broken ribs and muscles are a source of grief to me.

Well sneezing, it is terrible
it would bring you to your knees,
Sometimes your chest feels frozen
it is not a nice place to be.
For I think a good description
if my feelings I discussed,
Would be eaten by a shark and run over by a bus.

Now you have to take control of things
And steady up your head,
For suddenly you have lots of time doing nothing is a dread,
So I try to take it easy
And permit myself to mend
You just have to go along with it
that's the path I'd recommend.

Commercial Channel.

11th November Tuesday 2008.

In contrast to my feelings, to deny myself a film,
I decided I would break the rules
for once and take the helm,
So the other night was cold and wet
I had not much to do,
I sat myself upon the chair
and discarded both my shoes.

The film now I can't recall but it matters not for sure,
For when it all was over, I was ready for a cure,
I can't evoke if boredom
or frustration was the worst,
I only wish that those two hours
Could simply be reversed.

For the film was only started
when an advert hit the screen,
And it just went on for ever, bits of film in between,
We then returned to business
I tried hard to restore the plot,
But every thing I learned before, I simply just forgot.

So I stirred again my interest
and I soon became engrossed,
But before it all got going
I just give up the ghost,
For it was totally useless and my anger it was strong,
Trying to watch a broken movie
In between the Adverts Long.

Don't Blame God.

12th November Wednesday 2008.

I imagined myself one day to be God
looking through the paper,
The obituaries is my first port of call
I go through them with a scraper,
I'm hoping I won't miss someone
that I may just have known,
But mostly they're all strangers,
-- no relations of my own.

It's almost an obsession
when I think about it now,
For needing nothing else
I'll go for papers anyhow,
But usually and thankfully
most souls you've never met,
You can call that selfish – but
those names you just forget.

And then I thought could this be God
looking through the deaths,
Unfamiliar with the names of those
who've taken their last breaths?
And what an awesome thought to think
That God could feel the same,
"In life I never knew them
 But I was not to blame"

Dead Watch.

13th November Thursday 2008.

Johnny's watch was running slow
the reason why he did not know,
So when he past the jeweller's shop
to investigate he thought he'd stop,
He loosed his watch strap from his arm
and left it in the repair man's charm,
"I'll come back later when I get a chance
take the time for me and have a glance,
Hopefully you'll know what the problem is
for without that watch I cannot live".
Now the jeweller opened up Johnny's watch
while he sucked himself a butterscotch,
And there inside in the dust and the dirt
was a little black spider, the little squirt.
The jeweller decides that Johnny should be told
for the watch of course was many years old,
And the problem now, it was not only slow,
but the fact of the matter was, it would not go.
It would cost too much to try and repair
for it was the better for wear and tear,
So back Johnny came his watch to claim
only to find it was still the same,
"Sorry", says the jeweller, "there's nothing I can do
for the watch its as old as me and you,
But I did my best for the watch to test
It's in your hands now to do the rest",
But this for me was my biggest dread
For when I took off the back the
"The Driver Was Dead"

"POSH".

14th November Friday 2008.

There's a four letter word describes people with money,
It was always used in the land of honey,
Where people spent and forked out dosh
on trips and cruises, that word is <u>POSH.</u>

Here's how it came to get that name,
It was associated with those who had fame,
They could always afford and have more to spend
and so in a way the rules could bend.

Well the first two letters meant Port Side Out,
The side of the ship where the sun was about,
For the journey from here to American shores
you pay a little more where the sun shone more.

Well the port side out that meant south west,
It was the warmest side it was the best,
For a journey that lasted for a couple of weeks
it meant that you landed with rosy cheeks.

Well the last two letters meant Star Board Home,
When the ship turned round to sail the foam,
And the rich they all exchanged their beds
for the opposite side with the sun on their heads.

Now for them this side it was the best,
For although coming home it was still south west,
And when they landed on Ireland's shores
they were known as "<u>POSH</u>" in their pinafores.

Current Times.

15th November Saturday 2008.

There are certain things that we could blame
for changes in our time,
I will try to make examples with this simple little rhyme,
For instance take Electric, its ingenious you could say,
But without it think of all the things
we would not need today.

You would not need a microwave, a computer or TV,
You would not need a washing machine
or a dryer, don't you see,
And as for all the fridges and the freezers full of beef,
Without a flow of current
their life span would be brief.

You would not need those lights burning
inside your house or out,
You would not need a boiler pumping
water round your house,
Throw away your kettle and your iron to the bin,
The cooker and the hobs redundant items to throw in.

Well you could fill a lorry
full of articles rendered scrap,
Dispose of all the sockets,
all the switches, plugs and laps,
And just think of all the money
you could save for a rainy day,
If you hadn't all those units
of electric bills to pay.

Reflection.

'I searched for my soul, the soul I could not see,
I sought my God but my God eluded me
I searched for my brother and found all three'.

You can call this a reflection
Or you can call it a prayer
It is something that you can recite anywhere,
It was passed on to me
By a very good friend,
And onwards to you my best wishes extend.

It would not of course make everyone hoarse
To recite it would not be their scene
But it's certainly worth a moment of pause
To explore it up on the screen

For it says without brother is to be without God
And without brother is to be without soul
So if you have God and soul in your life
Then your brother is a sight to behold.

So in order for you to have both in your life
There's a few things you might need to do
Seek out the friends and the neighbours you have
And your relationship try to renew
For when you reflect it may just connect
That it's no where else to be found
The beauty of God and soul in man's eyes
It's there deep, and readily profound.

The Entrepreneur.

17th November Monday 2008.

What is it that makes an entrepreneur,
with the grizzle and the gravel
and the guts of a bear?
What is it that drives and motivates,
and makes them different, him and her?

What is it that makes an entrepreneur,
The challenge or the buzz
or the love affair?
That they all have with material things
and the fact that they are millionaires.

What is it that makes an entrepreneur,
With the problems and the worries
and times of despair?
What is it they have, that others lack
that steers them towards the silverware?

Well, the definition, I heard once,
of a hard wrought entrepreneur,
Someone who works sixteen hours a day,
for themselves no sweat they spare.

Because working eight hours every day
on premises employed by another,
Would not provide for them the thrill,
their lives would only smother.

Hay Making.

18th November Tuesday 2008.

When we were young in the summer days
we'd work with pitchforks turning hay,
Round and round the field we'd go
while the sun was scorching down below.

Our hands were blistered, sore and raw,
the wooden handles would sweat our paws,
And often we would run for shade
under an ash tree the sun would fade.

But first turn round was not too bad
for the hay was thick as was our dads,
But when it came to the second tilt
your back would break, your legs would wilt.

The fact that we were all so young
It made no difference you held your tongue,
And the only cure you had on a day
was when you turned around and smelt the tay.

Now that was always a sight to be seen
your ma with a kettle and sandwiches lean,
It made up for the chores we had to do
your problems died when she came in view,
And we'd all scramble like hungry hares
that bread and jam we all would share.

End Of An Era.

19th November Wednesday 2008.

Oh the axe has fallen on Woolworth's head
with soaring debts the banks have said,
No more excuses, we can't allow
we want our money and we want it now.

And jobs will go and heads will roll
and tears will shed in every ones soul,
Employees find themselves condemned
as Christmas comes their futures stemmed.

But competition is the name of the game
when it comes to money there is no shame,
It's just ruthless in the market place
the big boys always win the race.

Today it's the Woolworths and the MFI's,
tomorrow will bring more sad goodbyes,
A smaller slice of the apple pies
for the cake its self is still the same size.

But it is sad for the people out there
for the products were good the trade was fair
But the more we ship from foreign lands
the more we will leave redundant hands.

Still Of Night.

20th November Thursday 2008.

Oh the stillness of the night
when the moon is shining bright,
And the stars are gaping through
the frosty air,
There's a calmness in the shade
when the light begins to fade,
A time to have a kneel
and say a prayer.

Oh the silence is so serene
when it's windless in between,
All the noises and the rackets
of the day,
There's a quiet everywhere
and there's nothing to compare,
When every mouth is sealed
and tongues away.

Oh the peacefulness of night
which resembles candle light,
All the birds are resting
quiet in their nests
All the dogs are in their beds
all the people rest their heads,
A time like this when life
Is at its best.

Perfect Parents.

If the perfect parent could be found
then you would find the perfect child,
But until then it's doubtful
so you will have to wait a while.

For to find the perfect parent
could be difficult indeed,
It could be they're not invented yet
and maybe there's no such seed.

For to be the perfect parent
It could only mean one thing,
You'd have to come from perfect parents
whose lives resembled spring.

And again that could be doubtful
If the truth you had to bring,
For going back the generations
there was probably no such thing.

So we need to be contented
And just try to do our best,
For Imperfect parents and children
they can still be greatly blest.

"MUM".

22nd November Saturday 2008.

Forty years ago today
the sky fell black with grief,
For it was to our dear mother
that death came like a thief,
It stole her like a vulture
with no concern for us,
It hit her without warning
Its sting was venomous.

All those years have passed now
And still the blow is felt,
The pain is never ending
The sting of death is smelt,
She would not recognise us
If she came back today,
The world's a different place now
she has been so long away.

But since then our mum's in Heaven
she is sitting there tonight,
She travelled through the dark days
and fought the human fight,
And to all of us who knew her
and who loved her smile so well,
Will we meet her up in Heaven
or will we miss her down in Hell.

So let's get our act together,
If your life's being led astray,
It will definitely be possible,
for our Ma has paved the way.

The Unspeakable.

23rd November Saturday 2008.

When we were young we always had a toilet out the back,
There was no running water, or tissue paper on the rack,
The toilet had a bucket, galvanised to make it last,
And every day with ten of us, we filled it up so fast.

Now the bucket it was emptied away across the field,
It was a job that each of us was keen to keep concealed,
But it was common knowledge then and every body knew,
The neighbours all around us, sure they all did it too.

Sometimes we had to dig a hole to bury up the loot,
And this process for all of us was a topic for dispute,
It always created an argument as I remember now,
Just who had used the bog last, it always caused a row.

For the process it was simple when the bucket it was full,
You took your turn to empty it, 'twas not negotiable,
But sometimes it was left there, and allowed to overflow,
The culprits all abstaining from admitting to the woe.

Now all of us we took in turn the bum wipes to provide,
We'd tear the daily newspapers and hang them on a slide,
It meant you always had a read when sitting on the loo,
The neighbours all around us sure they all did it too.

My sister once was fussing and she flew into a rage,
The only sheet was left it had Cliff Richard on the page,
And being a fan for many years was pain for our wee lass,
She said she'd never use it, to clean and wipe her ass.

Generous To A Fault.

Years ago there was a man that I was pleased to know,
His problem was that every day he'd travel to and fro,
The journey it remained the same, on every single day,
He headed to the public house to drink his life away.

Well he never had a penny or a pound note to his name,
But he could always sit and drink his whiskeys all the same,
And his life was always miserable, his spirits always low,
Some said he was disgusting he would drink it from a poe.

He'd go down on a Monday and collect his local dole,
And then proceed to wash it all, down his watering hole,
It never was a problem meeting friends to quench his thirst,
When it came to generosity this man was always first.

But Monday came and Monday went, Tuesday was the same,
Every time I saw him sure it was an awful shame,
In fact sometimes I'd nearly cry to watch him crawling home,
Back inside, to those four walls, where he was all alone.

But nothing could be done for him and no one had a cure,
He was an alcoholic and his life was insecure,
He was under pressure in his mind he'd always think,
The hardest thing for him today was getting another drink.

Well that is how I knew him, yet he was very kind,
He never got in trouble with the law that I can mind,
But all the harm he done in life was always to himself
He died in total conflict with the bottle and his health.

"Christians".

25th November Tuesday 2008.

They were all in there together
In among the congregation,
They were making noise together
Breed, seed and generation,
And not a hand was lifted to eradicate the noise,
This family of youngsters all them girls and boys.

Well they brought along their toy cars
which they scrapped across the seats,
They brought along their cuddly dolls,
their chewing gum and sweets,
And nothing could be heard when the Gospel it was read,
This family they had voices big enough to wake the dead.

They would all climb up together
and annoy you in the pew,
And mummy would not say a word
as sweets and gum they chewed,
They'd poke you in the back and even try to pull your hair,
While you'd be trying hard for sure, trying not to swear.

But your tongue is firmly knotted
and you cannot say a word,
You give them all a little smile
While you whisper "that little turd"
And in your mind you ponder
why they cannot stay at home,
It would make us Christians happy
Just to be here on our own.

Captured.

26th November Wednesday 2008.

I can repeat a conversation
but I can't repeat a poem,
And strange enough as that may seem
It is actually now well known.

For all those in conversation
they just spread the news around,
Whether it be scandal
of some people round the town.

And you know what passes onwards
It gets greater all the time,
If some person won a hundred
the amount would always climb.

And so a conversation it travels everywhere,
It passes on to people, whether harsh or fair,
And mostly it's repeated on from ear to ear,
If there's something to be told
then folks will want to hear.

But when you write a poem
It is chiselled out in stone,
There may be people with opinions
to condemn it or condone,
But you never can repeat it
For the pen it never lies,
It will never be the same again
No matter how you try.

The Wife.

27ᵗʰ November Thursday 2008.

Dear Lord, this charming woman
who is beside me everyday,
You crafted up and moulded up
and pottered up like clay,
You sent her on a journey
and I know it was to be,
For I was very lucky
that she ended up with me.

Dear Lord, this woman is exquisite
she's unique, I have to say,
I know when you had made her
that you threw the plans away,
For she is such a prototype,
perfection made from scratch,
To try and find a pair of her
there would never be a match.

Dear Lord, it's really so important
for a man to have in life,
A very special woman
that he can call his wife,
For she can be his guidance
she can challenge him each day,
So keep making all those one offs
And the men won't go astray.

"Anguish".

28th November Friday 2008.

I grieve for people I do not know,
their sadness fills my heart,
I try to share their agony
but not knowing where to start.
For the roads they spell disaster
and it brings much family pain,
There is no way to express it
and no words that can explain.

For today there's another tragedy, yesterday was the same,
Two children on the roadside,
yet they were not to blame,
It is what we call an accident, and it happens all the time,
Today the hundredth victim
a wee girl in all her prime.

Well I do not know the answer, but it is not an act of God,
For I am sure that he is weeping
In his heart, is pierced a sword,
But I know that this could happen, I am guilty to the bone,
For sometimes when I'm driving
my instincts I disown.

But there are no words of comfort,
to relieve these parents grief,
There are simply some good actions
that will bring them sure relief,
But the pain will last forever, it will never go away,
We should remember them for always,
When we kneel down to pray.

The Twins.

29th November Saturday 2008.

Oh, Saturday in November
the day it was the eighth,
When early in the morning time
good news to celebrate,
For coming six weeks early
two girls they could not wait,
They had it in their minds for us
that they would not be late.

And so it was the twins were born,
our phones were all red hot,
At five a.m. before the dawn
God give them both a slot,
The phone it rang, the mobiles sang,
the news was soon in place,
The waiting now was over,
both mum and kids were safe.

Three weeks have passed them by now
both girls are thriving fast,
The families all are guessing
who they resemble from the past,
But it's all in conversation
and it's just a bit of crack,
For the truth is that they're gorgeous,
In their cots there, back to back.

Be A Devil.

30th November Sunday 2008.

The man that never made a mistake
In his life has made nothing at all,
He maybe could try to convince you he has,
but in truth he's still learning to crawl.

So if you are afraid of a trivial risk
or something that's relatively small,
Then make a decision to give it a go
and don't worry if you have to sprawl.

For all of us we have to make judgements,
It's as important as washing your face,
You get on the ride and finally decide
and you live it, with resolute pace.

So the longer the years you are living
then it's likely you'll make more mistakes,
So it's certain throughout the whole process,
There'll be plenty of chances to take.

Well the advice that I would be giving,
If your interest it is so inclined,
Tackle all that you can when you're living,
before the time comes to resign.

December

Titles Of Poems	*Month of December*		
"The Race"	1st December	Monday	2008
A Better Man	2nd December	Tuesday	2008
To Hell And Back	3rd December	Wednesday	2008
Take A Wee Look	4th December	Thursday	2008
"Cowboys"	5th December	Friday	2008
Donkey Derby	6th December	Saturday	2008
Kick It Now	7th December	Sunday	2008
Christmas Carol	8th December	Monday	2008
Spending Spree	9th December	Tuesday	2008
Inner Voice	10th December	Wednesday	2008
"Ignatius"	11th December	Thursday	2008
Lonely Face	12th December	Friday	2008
The Slow Down	13th December	Saturday	2008
Away In A Manger	14th December	Sunday	2008
Christmas Spirits	15th December	Monday	2008
Bleak December	16th December	Tuesday	2008
Chocoholic	17th December	Wednesday	2008
Good Days Bad Days	18th December	Thursday	2008
Spare A Thought	19th December	Friday	2008
Santa's Coming	20th December	Saturday	2008
Christmas Repentance	21st December	Sunday	2008
Daddy Christmas	22ndDecember	Monday	2008
Santa Bee	23rd December	Tuesday	2008

Christmas Eve	24th December	Wednesday	2008
The Nativity	25th December	Thursday	2008
A Tribute To Joe	26th December	Friday	2008
Play Time	27th December	Saturday	2008
The Gift	28th December	Sunday	2008
"Lord"	29th December	Monday	2008
Facing the Unknown	30th December	Tuesday	2008
Day To Day Secrets	31st December	Wednesday	2008

"The Race".

Hello December, there's a furling left to go,
I have eleven now behind me
And the pace is getting slow,
The race is nearly over the course is near complete,
The run up now to Christmas
a challenge still to meet.

I have managed all the hurdles
the high ones and the low,
I've stayed up in the saddle, against the odds I know,
But I can see the finish now
the end it is in sight,
The victory of winning, will take me to new heights.

For I was not the favourite
when this big race began,
The odds against me winning, would suit a betting man,
For setting out to run this length
was a challenge much too far,
My New Year Resolution was a race to reach the stars.

And even if I had four legs
Instead of just the two,
I could have fallen anytime, and never made it through,
For the going it was rough and smooth
The ground was wet and dry,
Will I enter this race next year?
Sure I might give it a try.

A Better Man.

2ⁿᵈ December Tuesday 2008.

I was thinking back a month or two
would the days be long for me?
Should I always get up early
or should I stay in bed to three?
For it isn't always easy to occupy your time,
Especially with no buildings
or structural steel to climb.

But forty years of training
Is not easy to reverse,
And there's just no use in waiting
for the arrival of the hearse,
So I set the clock for seven
and I try to greet the day,
I take a sheet of paper
And just plan to pave the way.

Well that's what I've been doing
for the last six months or more,
I don't intend to sit around
and become this dreadful bore,
I just take the time to visit
do a good turn when I can,
And hopefully at the and of this
I'll be a better man.

To Hell And Back

He called with me today
as he was passing on his way,
I hadn't seen his face for many years,
So I asked him how he'd been
travelling through this time machine,
And when I finished sure
his eyes filled up with tears.

He said "I've been to hell and back
more times than you could guess,
The wife walked out and left me
and she left me in a mess",
She says "I'm taking everything
that my two hands can hold,
And everything I can't take
It's going to be sold".

So I thought "why did I ask him
oh my God I don't need this",
I stood there just in agony
as he went on to reminisce,
"She's taken all I ever had
she's skinned me to the bone".
He left me feeling guilty
wishing he would just go home.

Take A Wee Look.

Take a wee look down below
and gaze to where your toenails grow,
Cast your eyes where your navel lies
full of early morning fries,
And try hard not to be surprised.

Take a wee look down below
and stare to where your fag butts throw,
Cast your eyes over morning fries,
wave your toenails all goodbye,
And try hard not to be surprised.

Take a wee look down below
to where your spittle often goes,
Neck outstretched to miss the fries,
after one or two good tries,
And try hard not to be surprised.

Take a wee look down below,
And instantly you're going to know
you cannot see your toenails grow,
So cast your eyes where navel lies
full of early morning fries,
And try hard not to be surprised.

"Cowboys"

5ᵗʰ December Friday 2008.

Rules and regulations we need to have a few,
'Cause the world is full of cowboys
who don't care for me and you,
They will price up jobs for builders
who are keen to save on costs,
With no thoughts to health and safety
they just do not give a toss.

Well now some are inexperienced
they just do not have a clue,
They go to sites with gutties on,
their mobiles phones pursue,
They make it very difficult
for the good men to survive,
By offering stupid prices
They take short cuts skimp and skive.

Well this just causes problems
and accidents will occur,
Then the rules and regulations
on the good they will incur,
So let's get back to basics
where the men must learn a trade,
And keep them off the building sites
until they make the grade.

Donkey Derby

6th December Saturday 2008.

Do you remember back to Sports days,
when all of us had such fun?
We would saddle up the donkeys
for the Derby's we would run,
You climbed high in the saddle
feeling all of ten feet tall,
But before the race had started
you were sure to take a fall.

For the donkeys were notorious
they were stubborn to the core,
And sometimes in your efforts
you'd be feeling awful sore,
And just as you were started
you'd slide down the donkey's bum,
before the race got going
your ass would be just numb.

And sometimes he would kick you
right underneath your chin,
Don't stand behind a donkey
or you're never going to win,
Just climb back in the saddle
with the bruises, sores and all
And like myself in years to come
the memories you'll recall.

Kick It Now

7th December Sunday 2008.

Stop smoking for God's sake,
it will wreck your health,
Plus the fact they are stinking and ruin your wealth,
For the cost of a packet adds up every week,
It's a bit of a waste just to burn out your cheeks.

For the smoke it is sucked down into your lungs,
It leaves a brown film all over your tongue,
And on its way down, your tubes gather tar,
Right into your body your organs it scars.

Well I know they're a drug, an addict I've been
I could drag away forty a day at eighteen,
I was upwards on thirty before I seen the light,
Nineteen eighty one, on a cold winters night.

Well I just took the packet and said this is it,
I'll no more be a slave to this parcel of shit,
For the craving was stupid, the whip was your own,
Without coffin nails you just felt all alone.

Now I would be cheating and will have to admit,
I was not on my own, when I decided to quit,
For I got a hand more powerful than mine,
He labelled the packet "for your early shrine"
And ever since that I still trust in his ways,
I will do without fags for the rest of my days.

Christmas Carol.

8th December Monday 2008.

My mother loved that special carol
we sang at Christmas time,
See Amid the Winters Snow
sent shivers through our spine,
Especially so on Christmas Eve
with Santa on his way,
My mother's voice would echo out
to praise this special day.

Now we would all be tucked in bed,
excited as could be,
Hoping that our stockings
would be packed beneath the tree,
And every now and then you'd hear
our mother's voice so clear,
See Amid the Winters Snow
she sang it so sincere.

But very soon for all of us
our eyes would feel the weight,
You'd hear her sing a new hymn
"children dears, its awful late,
If you are not all sleeping
when Santa Claus comes round,
He won't come down the chimney
if he hears the slightest sound".

Spending Spree

9th December Tuesday 2008.

Christmas is coming and the shops are full of stock,
Everybody's buying up to fill it in their socks,
The more you have the merrier,
the spending spree goes on,
Forget about recession 'til the money is all gone.

For what's the use in worrying
when you still have cash to spend,
What's the use in saving it,
sure the banks are going to lend,
And what's the use in leaving it
to join tomorrows fate,
Enjoy yourself at present'
for tomorrow could be too late.

It would seem this is the attitude
around this time of year,
When everybody's mission
Is to buy with out no fear,
And giving other presents
that we know we'll never need,
It seems like self indulgence
which we never seem to heed.

So lighten Santa's burdens, try it out this year,
Just cut down on the shopping especially the beer,
There is no need to panic, meet yourself halfway,
Leave some for tomorrow and shop another day.

Inner Voice.

10th December Wednesday 2008.

Your conscience is the driving force as life takes you along,
It forces you to think about what's
right and what is wrong,
It asks you to examine which direction you should take,
And in the end will influence
the decisions you will make.

For no matter how you try today your conscience will dictate,
It will not go away from you
and it never will be late,
You have to give it pride of place there is nothing you can do,
For no matter where you travel
your conscience will follow you.

For we have arms and legs and feet, a mouth a nose and ears,
And parked up in the middle
two eyes that fill with tears,
A heart, a soul, a body and a brain that's out of sight,
But most of all a conscience that makes us do what's right.

For nothing can suppress it
when it's alert and wide awake,
It will always try to shock us
and into better people make,
For it's always on the rampage, it's light is shining bright,
Take time to know the difference
If you are wrong or right.

"Ignatius"

11th December Thursday 2008.

Ignatius was an ignorant man, his nickname was brute force,
He used to shove his weight around
And he lived without remorse.

He could never find a minute, to explain to those around,
He was always in a panic
Like a hunting beagle hound.

He expected everyone to read his thoughts and pick his brain,
He was described by many as a man who was insane.
But down the years Ignatius, he was just like all the rest,
The years they wore away at him and put him to the test.

For though his strength was broken,
his tongue was still the same
And of course when something happened
everybody was to blame.

Well this man he never married, it was not part of his plan
He could not share his home place, never mind the land.
He lived with his wee sister,
she just cleaned and cooked and fed,
And when his health grew weaker
she attended him in bed.

Well Ignatius was impatient, but nature took its course,
His sister's life was easy, for he lost all his brute force,
But she was heard to say one day,
As his strength was now all gone,
Relief for poor Ignatius
But his ignorance it lived on.

Lonely Face.

12th December Friday 2008.

If you are feeling lonely,
conversation on your mind,
You are full of empty spaces
and dull moments of all kind,
You feel the need to have a chat,
to lighten up your day,
But there's no one all around you
Everybody's far away.

If you are feeling lonely,
conversation on your mind,
Try to take the first step
maybe you need to unwind,
Don't wait until a visitor
should come and knock your door,
Try to make a first move
some friendship to restore.

If you are feeling lonely,
conversation on your mind,
But still you find it difficult,
You're just not that way inclined,
Pay a visit to a graveyard,
to that quiet lonely place,
It's there you're sure to recognise
some other lonely face.

The Slow Down.

13th December Saturday 2008.

Christmas is overshadowed by the economic gloom,
There is little time for Jesus in an economic boom,
And yet it seems when all of us
should try to seek him more,
Christmas is overtaken by reductions in the stores.

In the midst of unemployment and recession every day,
The focus is on everything except the need to pray,
There's a growing consternation
and a void in peoples lives,
Waiting for the postman, the bills that will arrive.

Well this has been the worst one, for many, many years,
There is no doubt about it, you can't ignore the fears,
And it's just affecting everyone,
the knock on path kicks in,
Things could get much worse before
the good times they begin.

Now when we're spending money, large or be it small,
It's always helping someone, set up a market stall,
For all of us in some way
depend on others for our food,
It's in giving and in taking
that makes our world so good.

Away In A Manger

14th December Sunday 2008.

'Away in a Manger' is a lovely little hymn,
It's especially good for children
who are struggling to begin,
For the words are very simple
saying Jesus has no bed,
With the donkeys in a stable,
he has to lay his head.

The teacher she was patient
as she took them through the song,
But somewhere in the middle
she just knew someone was wrong,
So she asked this little fellow,
who was trying to do his best,
To take three paces forward
and to sing it for the rest.

Well the wee lad was delighted
and with confidence he sang,
His courage was amazing
as he faced his whole school gang,
But very soon the teacher knew
Just what was going wrong
"The kettle it is boiling"
he was singing in the song.

Christmas Spirits.

15th December Monday. 2008.

Christmas time, lemon and lime,
Bacardi and coke, and nickels and dimes,
Scotch on the rocks, people get blocked,
Whiskey and water, and no-one is shocked.

Brandy and beer, a great atmosphere,
Ballygowan water, for pioneers here,
Red wine and white wine, fill up your glass
Sing and be merry, while all of this lasts.

A stout and a Guinness
It resembles sweet milk
Your taste buds are smoothing, feeling of silk,
A harp and a lager, to wash it all down
Gradually now you'll be acting the clown.

A tonic and gin will do to begin,
The thrist it will soon pass me by,
At the end of the night, if I want to be tight
I can always drink Canada dry.

Bleak December.

16th December Tuesday 2008.

December now is halfway through,
can the news get any bleaker?
It would seem against the euro
that the pound is getting weaker.
The economy is in turmoil,
buying money is the game,
There are firms going out of business
a recession's hard to tame.

But it's coming up to Christmas,
on December the twenty fifth,
We need to all be positive
just to give our lives a lift,
Don't forget the celebration
do not be without the hope,
Please prepare for this new baby,
he will stop this sliding slope.

For all of us we climbed on board
this roller coaster ride,
We were all going round in circles,
we were blind and bleary eyed,
For joining in the rat race
Is the natural thing to do.
We don't expect to hit the bottom
even with the birds eye view.

Chocoholic.

17th December Wednesday 2008.

I don't know why or what it is, when you eat a chocolate sweet,
There's this craving for another one
in that box of Quality Street,
I am now convinced that there's a drug
in all this chocolate stuff,
One sweet is far too many and a hundred not enough.

When I eat a square of chocolate, I can't forget the taste
The enzymes in my brain keep saying
Eat the rest in haste,
Especially the Milk Tray, it slips down honey sweet,
And the craving for another one
You simply can't defeat.

Well I remember back in years when chocolate was a treat,
You maybe got a Milky Way or a Mars Bar to eat,
A little box of Roses were delicious on your tongue,
But it never seemed to torture us
when we were very young.

But nowadays it's different,
the ingredients must be rigged,
It definitely is addictive you could eat it like a pig,
For when a box is opened you just have to scoff the lot,
One flavour on your lips and you are hooked there on the spot.

Now what it is, I do not know, what's in this chocolate stuff,
One sweet is far too many and a thousands not enough,
So if you're a chocoholic and you just indulge yourself,
Take my advice and listen,
Just leave them on the shelf.

Good Days, Bad Days.

18th December Thursday 2008.

There will always be good days,
there will always be bad,
no matter if your sick or well,
What can happen over the course of an hour,
you just can never tell,
For your state of affairs can always change
at any time of the day,
In a sudden shift of fortunes
you could head in a different way.

Now the map that most of us follow
Is one designed by ourselves,
The plan that we sometimes swallow
Is disguised by our own selfish smells,
For we do not expect a diversion
from all of the things that we do,
But all of know just from living
that change can come out of the blue.

At ten you could be on top of the world
at noon the world it could stop,
For an act of God, or nature it's self
could push you over the top,
For nothing is plain or simple no more
and anger is always so strong,
There's always a reason for being upset
when everything seems to go wrong.

It's rarely that we're ever contented
there's a longing for a little bit more,
There's a feeling of a day that is wasted
if achievements don't darken our door,
But there will always be good days and bad days
despite what we have or have not,
So take time to appreciate fully,
The Life you already have got.

Spare A Thought.

19th December Friday 2008.

For many people Christmas day will be a lonely time,
Lives that have been wrecked
with deaths and robberies and crimes,
Weeks and months of suffering
and days that bring despair,
A Christmas without meaning
at the sight of an empty chair.

The car it just went off the road we lost our only son,
For many people, Christmas
will be a lonely one,
The old man in his ninety's
worn out with all the years,
They stole his small possessions
and they left his life in tears.

Then there are those people, their sons locked up in jails,
For them a time of agony
asking where they failed,
There seems to be no answers
the suffering shared between,
The families of the victims
with the families shame has seen.

So spare a thought at Christmas, partake in peoples' pain,
Remember those especially
at the point of sheer insane,
For troubles never pick and choose
just where they aim to land,
And usually for the most of us
It's trouble that's unplanned.

Santa's Coming.

20th December Saturday 2008.

Santa Claus is coming, ring the chimney sweep today,
For the soot is awful dirty
and it's a narrow passageway,
And Santa Claus is very fat
his suit is red and white,
He cannot be untidy when he comes tomorrow night.

Don't forget to damp the fire and empty out the grate,
When Santa comes and sees it
he will sure appreciate,
Your toys will all be tidy
when he stacks them by the tree,
And don't forget to leave for him a little cup of tea.

He also likes a biscuit and a little glass of wine,
But please be careful not to leave
too much for him to dine,
For he is going onwards
more visits he must make,
It's really so important that he isn't running late.

Well don't forget the thank you cards
for all the lovely toys,
Santa loves to read them
from all the girls and boys,
And make a little room for him
around the chimney breast,
for he must make a speedy exit
to bring gifts to all the rest.

Christmas Repentance.

21st December Sunday 2008.

People go to make confessions
around this Christmas time,
They go to get the pot scraped,
to remove the slime and grime,
It's traditionally for Catholics, a sacrament of grace,
Where sins are all forgiven and another year to face.

Some people say it's crucial
to remove the stains of guilt,
And once a year is not enough
your memory to jilt,
But Christmas time is usually, a time when most repent,
A time when Heaven opens, and our Saviour Jesus sent.

Well maybe it is worthwhile
to leave it all behind,
And tell yourself that God above
forgives all humankind,
Why carry all this baggage
when confession wipes the slate,
Maybe you should do it now,
before it is too late.

Now there are some opinions
which can vary all the while,
Some go to make confessions
and return home with a smile,
And some they see psychologists
and they whimper all their cares,
So you can chose yourself just where
you rest your soul's affairs.

Daddy Christmas.

22nd December Monday 2008.

My Da, he was an honest man, he died without a shilling,
No matter what he worked at
he could never make a killing,
But he was always decent
and his life was simply lived,
On every opportunity he would reach his hand and give.

He never owned a motor car, and he never owned a house,
He always hired his labour
and my mother was his spouse,
He reared us all on buttons
but we never went without,
When it came to our religion, they always were devout.

Now when it came to Christmas time
and Santa was his role,
He always made an effort,
he left us his heart and soul,
Extravagance was not in sight
but Santa Claus was good,
Looking back we never,
could have fully understood.

For how they made those ends meet
I just will never know,
They could serve us up from nothing
till our hearts would overflow,
And in his life of giving
he was full of good advice:
"Choose a decent woman
if you're looking for a wife".

Santa Bee.

23rd December Tuesday 2008.

If Santa Claus was a bumble Bee
he could travel all over the globe,
He could carry his toys tucked under his wings,
and his presents tied under his robe.

He would have no need for a reindeer,
and the sleigh he could leave in the shed,
With the wings that's attached to his body
he could fly down the chimney instead.

If Santa Claus was a bumble Bee
he could bring us gifts of honey,
With scented smell and fragrance
would he give his children money?
He would fill our lives with pollen
and with nectar he would mix,
And then each year at Christmas time
our selfish hearts he'd fix.

But Santa Claus is not a Bee
and honey he cannot make,
And flying all around the world
is a journey he cannot take,
But deep inside each one of us
where Santa dwells so deep,
There lie the seeds of many gifts
that each of us can reap.

Christmas Eve.

24th December Wednesday 2008.

When you're laying in your bed tonight
this blessed Christmas eve,
Your mind is racing onwards,
to the gifts you will receive,
The wind it may be howling
and the snow flakes falling down,
But you just know for certain,
Santa Claus will be around.

For it has been a year now
since you felt this way before,
It's simply sheer excitement, waiting for your toys galore.
You have written all your letters
and you posted them in hope,
That everything you asked for, how will poor Santa cope?

But cope he will, your stockings fill,
his word is always true,
For Mummy, Daddy said so sure you know they always do
And when the night is silent
and your dreams are all so real,
St Nicholas will be working hard, his reindeer sleigh to sail.

And in the hours of darkness
when the world is out of sight,
The presents and the parcels
will be left throughout the night,
Then wake up in the morning
and fill the house with cheers,
"Mummy, Mummy, Daddy look,
Santa Claus -- was here".

The Nativity.

On Christmas day we celebrate the birth of Jesus Christ
He was born of the Virgin Mary
and conceived in Paradise,
The message came from Gabriel,
sent down from heaven above,
God chose this single lady and filled her with his love.

Well Mary she was terrified, this news was scary stuff,
How can I be a mother
sure my life is rough enough?
But the Angel he consoled her
that the baby would be born,
That God would not forsake her amidst the thorn of scorn.

Well Joseph was her boyfriend bequeathed to take her hand,
This news was so upsetting
and he had to take a stand,
But the Angel reassured him
to stay by Mary's side,
God had a plan for both of them
his strength he would provide.

And so it was it came to pass two thousand years ago,
He has taken us through centuries
of war and strife and woe,
But for those of us who listen
and his message take on board,
His promise is eternity
and a life still unexplored.

A Tribute to Joe.

26th December Friday 2008.

I want to write a poem about a very famous Joe,
He captivated most of us all those years ago,
And for some of us it seemed unreal, that Joe had passed away,
He died, 'twas on St Stephen's day, a year ago today.

But Joe he was our hero "In his own peculiar way"
He was "The answer to everything" in
"The Games that people play"
When he sang "Unchained Melody"
"My First Love" came in view
And I remember saying "It's you, It's you, It's you".

For all of us at dances simply wanted "More and More"
I remember "Crazy Woman", "Sister Mary" was in store,
And when he sang that lovely song
"Aching Breaking Heart"
"Sweet little rock in roller" surly tore your heart apart.

"Sometimes a Man just has to cry" was real a year ago,
When God said Joe "Come Back Home"
It was an awful blow,
"The house with the whitewashed gable"
And the road of "Tar and Cement"
That golden voice of Ireland, it was only out on rent.

Joe was the "love of the common people"
"His first Love was never to be"
for "You're such a good looking woman"
And "Theresa" he always could see,
For all of us who follow "We can't help falling in love"
"Those pretty brown eyes" they are resting

With Joe the great Dolan above.

Play Time.

27ᵗʰ December Saturday 2008.

The children were excited
when the gifts were all unwrapped,
Especially the little ones
who screamed and cried and clapped,
With the paper torn apart and the boxes thrown aside,
they would shout with great commotion,
little minds so occupied.

With the toys of all descriptions
sure they don't know where to look,
They'd start off with a teddy bear,
and end up with a book,
And maybe they would play a while
with a cuddly woollen fox,
It wasn't long before the crack
came from the empty box.

And when the afternoon is gone,
the turkey gone as well,
You're sitting round the sofa
with your belly full and swelled,
And all the toys are gathered up
discarded round the fire,
They are sitting watching telly
with all their hearts desire.

For children's concentration only lasts a little while,
They need a parent's guidance to share a loving smile,
For Santa's gifts are useless if Mummy doesn't play,
And Daddy kicking football
will make his children's day.

The Gift.

28th December Sunday 2008.

I thought about giving my wife a gift
something that belonged to my Ma,
It seemed like a good idea for once
although you might think it bizarre,

But over the years
I have been with the bride,
and from the very first moment we met,
She never was fortunate
to meet with my Ma,
and for me that's an awful regret.

For loosing your Ma
when you're young in your life,
Is a blow that's beyond all repair,
For it means when you meet
a wee girl of your own,
that you don't have a mother to share,

But luxuries were never
a part of my home,
and my mother was short in supply,
Sometimes when I think of how little she had
my eyes just refuse to stay dry.

So for me to bequeath a wee gift to my wife,
Something that belonged to my Ma,
I will have to deliver this gift of my life,
In all of our beautiful Ba's.

"Lord".

29th December Monday 2008.

You are my source of comfort, Lord,
you are my saving grace,
In times when I ignore you,
you will always give me space,
And when I think I'm ready
to return to see your face,
You are there with ears wide open,
for me to plead my case.

You are my source of joy, Lord,
In you I find my soul,
In times when I disown you,
you still offer me parole,
And when I think I'm sinning
and I want to take a stroll,
You are there with arms wide open,
reaching out to make me whole.

You are my source of light, Lord, in you I take my rest,
In times when I feel near you,
you don't put me to the test,
And when my body's tired, Lord, with feelings of unrest,
You are there with all your angels,
calling me to be your guest.

You are my source of light, Lord, my flash lamp in the dark,
In times when I can't see you,
you will always leave a spark,
And when I stumble over, and I grasp for Noah's ark,
You are there with eyes wide open,
saving me from all the sharks.

Facing the Unknown

30th December Tuesday 2008.

We have no way of knowing
what each new year will bring,
We have no way of telling
what will happen in the spring,
But each of us in planning
we should always keep in mind,
The trials and tribulations
in the year we left behind.

We have no way of knowing
who'll be here two thousand and nine,
We have no way of telling
just who will walk the line,
For each of us we follow
in the ways that we know best,
We will go in all directions
be it north, south, east or west.

Well no-one can predict for us, the future is unsure,
And no-one can return to us the year that's just matured,
For all that's happened gone now
and it never will return,
A new year lies ahead of us to face without concern.

So let us all look forward in an optimistic way,
Let us face the future and just take it day by day,
There is no use in worrying,
It is out of our control,
We cannot change one minute
when the New Year all unfolds.

Day To Day Secrets.

31ˢᵗ December Wednesday 2008.

December is nearly over now and the year is almost gone,
I have shared with you my secrets
It has been a marathon,
And with out the shear commitment it refused to let me go,
My New Year Resolution would have died a death you know.

But looking back I'll never fully truly understand
What kept the passion going, my pen so close at hand,
And during the terrible bad times
when life it seemed so frail,
The writing saved my sanity
And I lived to tell the tale.

For sickness is a burden and illness bogs you down,
In fact at times you really think
the world has stopped going round,
Some days don't have a meaning
there are empty hours to spend,
At certain times you could not care if life came to an end.

But then you get a door knock, a friend is standing there,
A neighbour or a colleague someone who really cares,
And suddenly in hope and love, the truth you realise,
How great and good and special that it is to be alive.

For I have witnessed angels, and saints come to the fore,
My family and relations stood by me all the more,
The doctors and the nurses
all the staff who shared their love,
I dedicate this poem
And commend you all to God above.

Printed in the United Kingdom by
Lightning Source UK Ltd., Milton Keynes
139213UK00002B/2/P